REFRAMING WRITING ASSESSMENT

kis

REFRAMING WRITING ASSESSMENT TO IMPROVE TEACHING AND LEARNING

LINDA ADLER-KASSNER
PEGGY O'NEILL

UTAH STATE UNIVERSITY PRESS
Logan, Utah
2010

Utah State University Press
Logan, Utah 84322-7800

ISBN 978-0-87421-798-8 (paperback)
ISBN 978-0-87421-799-5 (ebook)

Manufactured in the United States of America
Cover photo and design by Barbara Yale-Read

Library of Congress Cataloging-in-Publication Data
Adler-Kassner, Linda.
Reframing writing assessment to improve teaching and learning / Linda Adler-Kassner,
Peggy O'Neill.
p. cm.
Includes bibliographical references and index.
ISBN 978-0-87421-798-8 (pbk. : alk. paper) – ISBN 978-0-87421-799-5 (e-book : alk. paper)
1. English language–Rhetoric–Study and teaching. 2. Grading and marking (Students) 3.
Report writing–Evaluation. 4. College prose–Evaluation. I. O'Neill, Peggy - II. Title.
PE1404.A347 2010
808'.0420711–dc22
                    2010010079

CONTENTS

ACKNOWLEDGMENTS

We first began collaborating as part of the Network for Media Action, a component of the Council of Writing Program Administrators dedicated to developing strategies for program directors and writing instructors to participate in public conversations about writing. CWPA and the WPA-NMA have provided a hospitable, engaging, and supportive community of fellow writing instructors and program directors. This book came out of generative conversations with colleagues from that organization, including Dominic Delli Carpini, Darsie Bowden, Eli Goldblatt, and others. Once we started thinking about developing our ideas on reframing into a book, Leasa Burton encouraged us to create an initial proposal. We would like to thank the reviewers for USUP who pushed and prodded us to do more and the participants at various conference workshops and presentations who were the initial audiences for several parts of the manuscript, providing valuable feedback as we worked through ideas and drafts. A special thanks to the colleagues who participated in our research by sharing their experiences with us through interviews and documents. Thanks also to our colleagues and friends, both near and far, who read drafts of different parts of the manuscript, provided feedback, and helped us along the way—especially , Bill Smith, Susanmarie Harrington, Brian Huot, Cathy Fleischer, and the USUP anonymous reviewers. Finally, thanks to Michael Spooner and others at USUP who continued to encourage and support us through the various stages of publishing. And of course, thanks to our families, who listen to and live with us as we work every day.

1

HIGHER EDUCATION, FRAMING, AND WRITING ASSESSMENT

Consider the following scenario, discussed on the Writing Program Administration listserv (WPA-L). The scenario is based on the experiences of a writing program administrator at a large midwestern university:

> The writing program director learns that "there is a movement afoot" at her university to administer the Collegiate Learning Assessment (CLA) to first-year students and seniors. This will mean that these students will take a ninety-minute essay exam designed to "test" their critical thinking skills. The tests results will be published so that her institution can be compared to others in its category and, if necessary, used to improve any weaknesses that are identified.

In listening to the conversations on campus, this program director feels there is an implicit message that the test would be a way of marketing the school as a "first-rate institution." Although no one explicitly discusses the CLA as an assessment of writing (instead, they say, it is an indication of critical thinking skills), she feels strongly that it will reflect on the writing program.

In response to what she is learning as she listens to the discussions on campus, the program director turns to the national community of writing professionals on the WPA-L to get background information for her upcoming meeting with the university assessment committee. She learns that the test is just one indicator the school wants to use to demonstrate "critical thinking"—although the other indicators were never articulated, at least not to her. After the meeting, she writes a memo to the committee and administrators outlining her concerns based on her knowledge of writing pedagogy, assessment, and the curriculum at her institution. The memo outlines the disadvantages of the test and the possibilities of developing an in-house assessment. This type of assessment, she argues, would better serve the needs of the local institution and would be more likely to improve teaching and learning. By her own admission, she doesn't know if this detailed memo (almost three pages long) will do any good. However, much later, she learns that the CLA was abandoned, but she doesn't know why. She "heard that one of the administrators who was involved in this mentioned" that her "memo was 'unhelpful.'" None of her suggestions for a locally designed assessment that would track students across their undergraduate careers was adopted—nor was it even discussed seriously at the time, she admits. In her words, the CLA "threat" just went away. In the end, she has ideas about the motivation behind the initial move, but she has no concrete evidence. The writing program does do ongoing program review, and it has always been praised by the administration for that review. As the program director, she wasn't aware of the conversations about using writing as way to assess critical thinking at the university level, and she wasn't brought into the deliberations. She did, however, react to the news and provide her perspective as the program director and a composition scholar.

This example, which has been repeated in various permutations in listserv discussions, in hallway conversations at conferences, and on campuses across the country, illustrates the dilemmas and questions that can emerge around assessment. While the example reflects the experiences of many writing instructors, program directors, department chairs, or other writing professionals, it represents just one type of assessment—institutionally based, university-wide assessment—about which we hear fairly often. As the example also illustrates, the extent to which we writing professionals are "included" (asked or invited to participate; directed to provide input) in these discussions varies, sometimes from moment to moment or day to day.

We know that all postsecondary educators live in a culture where assessment is increasingly important. From the nearly ubiquitous process of program review to assessments (also) linked to accreditation to institutional participation in initiatives like the Voluntary System of Accountability (VSA, which might involve administration of one of three standardized tests: the Collegiate Assessment of Academic Progress [CAAP], Measure of Academic Progress and Proficiency [MAPP], or the Collegiate Learning Assessment [CLA]; or might involve use of the AAC&U's VALUE rubrics), the sheer number of efforts—and acronyms—surrounding assessment can be at best incredibly confusing, and at worst positively dizzying. Whether a classroom instructor, a course director, someone who works with a writing program, or someone who serves in some other teaching and/or administrative capacity on campus, it's likely that all of us have dealt with some kind of assessment scenario in our courses, programs, or institutions. Often these writing assessments are locally designed and administered, but they can be part of the alphabet soup that marks the national standardized testing marketplace. Conversations also frequently include exams more directly connected to writing programs, such as the SAT Writing Test, ACCUPLACER, COMPASS , E-rater, or even AP or CLEP exams.

Regardless of the end point or process used, three very broad questions can be asked about assessments:

1. What is the purpose of an assessment?
2. Who is (or are) the primary audience(s) for an assessment and its results?
3. What decisions might, or will, result from an assessment?

Within these broad questions, a number of others are also present: What assessments are appropriate, and why? What will be the relationship between assessment and curriculum? Who will determine what assessment(s) will be used, when, and how? How will the assessment results be interpreted, communicated, and used? More importantly, how do faculty—whether classroom instructors, directors of writing programs or centers, department chairs, or any other interested faculty—get involved in these discussions earlier than we so often do, hearing about them only as they drift down through campus administrators or conversations?

With so many different processes, programs, tests, and options, these discussions can be overwhelming and confusing. However, we believe they are currently not just important, but *the most important* discussions happening on our campuses (and even beyond them) today. They affect everything about our courses and programs—who is admitted to them; how they are taught; how students, courses, and instructor(s) are evaluated; what counts as valuable in them—in essence, everything that motivates writing instructors to do the work we do. For this reason, it is also crucial that postsecondary writing instructors and program directors get involved in assessment conversations, especially those that are explicitly about writing assessments (or are being used to make judgments about writing programs and student writing abilities).

This book is intended to help readers with that involvement. But as the vignette opening this chapter illustrates, "getting involved" isn't simply about administering a test or grading portfolios. It is about becoming immersed in discussions about teaching writing and learning to write, about who is doing the teaching and the learning, and ultimately, about how we define these activities. Increasingly, it is also about participating in an ever-widening series of conversations not just about composition but also about how people inside and outside the academy understand the purpose(s) of education, what those purposes have to do with visions of what it means to be a twenty-first-century citizen, and how all of this comes back to what students should learn—in postsecondary education generally, and in writing classes more specifically. Writing assessment, in other words, cannot be separated from these larger issues because these larger, contextual issues determine—whether directly or indirectly—much of what happens in postsecondary institutions and our programs and classrooms. Mike Rose makes this case with typical eloquence when he notes that "[i]t matters a great deal how we collectively talk about education, for that discussion both reflects and, in turn, affects policy decisions about what gets taught and tested, about funding, about what we expect schooling to contribute to our lives. It matters, as well, how we think about intelligence, how narrowly or broadly we define it" (2009, 5).

What we're saying, then, is that those discussions that we as two- or four-year college writing teachers or program directors might have about assessment—with other instructors in our program, with colleagues in our department, with campus administrators, or with people outside of our institutions—aren't *just* about writing assessment. Instead, they exist within an ever-expanding galaxy of questions (represented in Fig. 1) about what people need to know to "be successful" in the twenty-first century. These questions are inexorably linked to other items that populate the galaxy, as well—ideas about what it means to be a part of "America" as a country; ideas about how America develops as a nation and what is necessary for that to happen; ideas about how the nation's youth become "productive" citizens and what "productive" means.

Many, many different voices in this galaxy are attempting to weigh in on these discussions. Together, they embody the intrinsic relationship—sometimes implied, sometimes explicitly stated—between education and the nation's progress. Since the mid-nineteenth century (and even before), the idea that schooling should prepare students for participation in the broader culture has been a taken-for-granted purpose of education. Horace Mann, the "father" of the common school movement, reiterated this point frequently in his *Lectures on Education*, where he outlined four "powers and faculties" that education needed to take into account: a "moral" conscience shaped by allegiance to God; "social or sympathetic" sensibilities that came from ties to community; linkages to family and family traditions; and a self-focused set of behaviors (1891, 126–127). The role of education, in Mann's estimation, was to simultaneously appeal to

SITE OF INQUIRY
A. Classroom

PARTICIPANTS
students
instructor

SITE OF INQUIRY
B. Program

PARTICIPANTS
program director
all instructors
faculty beyond program

SITE OF INQUIRY
C. Department

PARTICIPANTS
department chair
all faculty in dept
faculty beyond dept
administrators

SITE OF INQUIRY
D. Institution

PARTICIPANTS
administrators
board of trustees/regents
alumni
community members

SITE OF INQUIRY
E. Community

PARTICIPANTS
employers
state legislators, dept of ed
community members

SITE OF INQUIRY
F. Specialty Accreditors

PARTICIPANTS
advisory boards
reviewers
faculty
students

SITE OF INQUIRY
G. Regional Accreditors

PARTICIPANTS
advisory boards
reviewers
U.S. Dept of Education

QUESTIONS RELATING TO SITES

A. What do students need to know or have experienced to participate as thoughtful, productive communicators? How can we improve their learning in this regard?

B. How can we work to improve students' critical writing, reading, and analysis strategies throughout our courses so they become thoughtful communicators?

C. How does the writing program and/or its courses contribute to the department's teaching and learning goals?

D. How does the writing program and its courses equip students with essential strategies or skills? To what extent does it do so successfully?

E. To what extent are graduates of the institution equipped with strategies and skills useful for community participation or career?

F. To what extent does the writing program and its courses, as part of an undergraduate education, contribute to students' preparation for a career in [X]?

G. To what extent does the writing program and its courses, as part of an education:
  - identify goals for and work to improve student learning
  - demonstrate how its goals are being accomplished
  - prove that students have [experienced, achieved, mastered] strategies essential for [citizenship, career, major]?

Fig. 1. "Galaxy" of Questions

these sensibilities and enable the nation's youth to shape them into behaviors that would advance what he saw as the nation's divinely inspired and fueled sense of mission.

Of course, literacy—both reading and writing—has long been considered a critical component of education. While it might seem an act of hubris on our part to situate writing instruction at the center of these ongoing conversations—after all, we are writing teachers and researchers ourselves—in fact, that is where policy reports and discussions about education place it, too. As a subject that is considered central to students' successes when they enter college, during postsecondary education, and into careers, writing is often a centerpiece of discussions about (and, sometimes, a prescription for) what should happen in secondary and postsecondary classrooms in order for students to be prepared for next steps. Influential reports like the American Diploma Project's *Ready or Not: Creating a High School Diploma that Counts,*[1] released electronically on the Achieve Web site in 2004, include dire proclamations about students' writing, like the warning that "[m]ore than 60 percent of employers question whether a high school diploma means that a typical student has learned even the basics, and they rate graduates' skills in grammar, spelling, [and] writing . . . as only 'fair' or 'poor'" (3). A discussion paper outlining the parameters of the Voluntary System of Accountability (VSA)[2] makes virtually

---

1. The American Diploma Project Network, a partnership among Achieve, Education Trust, the Thomas B. Fordham Foundation, and others, has worked in conjunction with the National Governors Association to "reform" secondary education. As of this writing, in thirty-five states that educate over 85 percent of the nation's high school students (achieve.org) have worked with ADP. Achieve, Inc. describes itself on its website as "an independent, bipartisan, non-profit education reform organization based in Washington, DC that helps states raise academic standards and graduation requirements, improve assessments, and strengthen accountability. In 2006, Achieve was named by *Education Week* as one of the most influential education groups in the nation."

2. The VSA is a national initiative of the Association of Public Land Grant Universities (APLU, formerly the National Association of State Universities and Land Grant Colleges [NASLGC] and the American Association of State Colleges and Universities [AASCU]) in which (as of this writing)

the same claim: "American companies report that many college graduates were lacking in . . . basic communication skills," including writing, and that 57 percent of "the public" said that "top-notch writing and speaking ability" is " 'absolutely essential' for higher education" (McPherson and Shulenberger 2006). These reports illustrate a refrain we often repeat when we talk about writing assessment with colleagues: writing is everyone's business. Everyone, however, doesn't agree on how to define "writing," let alone "good writing" or "writing ability." Likewise, everyone doesn't agree on what to teach or how to teach when it comes to writing. More importantly, at least from our perspective, not everyone has the same expertise and the same investment in writing instruction.

In other words, although we may all agree that writing "is not a frill for the few, but an essential skill for the many," as the National Commission on Writing in America's Schools and Colleges argues in its 2003 report, *The Neglected R: A Need for a Writing Revolution*, we don't necessarily agree on much beyond that. Employers, policymakers, and educators bring different experiences, expertise, agendas and commitments to the conversation. Within these broad groups, there are different perspectives that can represent disparate, even contradictory, views. The debate over reading instruction that swirled around Reading First legislation (and that ultimately played into No Child Left Behind, or NCLB) in the late 1990s, for instance, illustrates the high-stakes nature of these debates. The definition of what counted as "research"—"scientific study backed by quantitative data"— privileged phonics-based reading instruction (and research validating that approach) while discounting

---

"520 public institutions that enroll 7.5 million students and award 70% of bachelor's degrees in [the] U.S. each year" are currently participating (voluntarysystem.org). The VSA is intended to measure "value added" by a postsecondary education to skills considered essential for postsecondary success: critical analysis, written communication, and quantitative reasoning. VSA materials are careful to position this overall assessment as one intended to supplement, not replace, discipline-specific work (see McPherson and Shulenberger, 2007).

whole language instruction and research. While less high stakes (for now), a similar tension can be found in writing instruction, where there are often disagreements about the role of explicit grammar instruction in teaching writing. While most composition scholars trained in composition and rhetoric may agree that teaching grammar in isolation is not effective in improving students' written texts, there are many, many writing instructors who have not had the kind of graduate education that supports this approach. Even if official positions by professional organizations do not endorse grammar exercises as a best practice, many writing instructors do in practice and in public venues. In other words, within the population of those who identify as writing instructors, there is diversity of positions and practices.

So if "everyone" (and that's a big word, we realize) thinks writing is their business, how can we as college-level educators and scholars interact with them around these issues of writing assessment—issues, as we have indicated, that are related to considerably larger concerns and purposes, and about which there is sometimes considerable tension? That is the main question we take up in this book. Our position is that writing instructors and program directors know a lot about writing instruction and need to be centrally involved in discussions about writing assessment. Although not all writing professionals may agree on the particulars, by engaging in conversations about what we value, the purpose of education, and teaching practices, we can clarify some of the issues at the core of the assessment debate. We also believe the process we use to enter into and carry out these conversations is absolutely crucial and incredibly valuable. This book, then, is not an argument for taking a particular position in these discussions. Instead, it is an argument for *getting involved*—for working strategically, on our own and with others in our programs, institutions, and communities—in discussions about writing and writing assessment.

In writing this book we have two main purposes. First, we aim to convince readers—as individual professionals and as members of a profession—that we need to engage in these discussions about writing pedagogy and assessment wherever they might occur. Second, we provide readers with the necessary knowledge for engaging in these discussions. Our intention is not to tell readers what postsecondary instructors or administrators should say about writing instruction and assessment but to provide useful background knowledge and strategies for productive engagement in these discussions. Because we believe writing assessment is a powerful form of communication, we illustrate the strategies with real-world examples of writing program administrators and scholars engaging in writing assessments. We also report on professionals involved in writing assessment projects that move beyond their own campuses and into the broader context of higher education.

Chapter two, "Framing (and) American Education," opens with a discussion about the concept of frames and framing, the idea that there are conceptual and ideological boundaries shaping what is "common sense" and what is not. Then, proceeding from the idea that an understanding of the past is absolutely crucial to gain an understanding of the present (e.g., Schubert 1986, 54), we describe how American education in general has been framed historically. We then use this historical foundation as a basis to examine current-day framing of American education generally, and writing education specifically, to discuss the central challenges of reframing writing assessment—engaging in conversations that speak to a variety of audiences and address a number of purposes. Any effort to reframe writing assessment, we contend, must begin with a thorough understanding of framing and the current frame—otherwise, we run the risk of inadvertently perpetuating or contradicting elements of this frame in ways that might serve other purposes than those we intend.

In chapter three, "The Framing of Composition and Writing Assessment," we focus more specifically on the link between postsecondary writing instruction and writing assessment. Again, we begin with the past, examining ways that writing assessment has historically been framed and how that framing is linked to larger ideas about education and writing instruction. We also review some of the basics of approaches to composition (and assessment), including the rhetorical and sociolinguistic frames that inform contemporary writing pedagogy. By examining the psychometric frame that has dominated assessment, including writing assessment, we show how the story of writing assessment has been shaped by this frame. The basic premise underlying these two chapters is that we need to understand the past and present as we look to the future. Once we understand the frames already in place, we can begin to develop ways to build on these structures, to reframe writing and writing assessment in a way that will support our values and beliefs.

Chapter four, "Reframing Strategies and Techniques," presents useful, hands-on strategies for reframing work. These strategies begin with alliance building and extend to communicating with a range of audiences. Underscoring this chapter is the idea that we must act strategically if we want to reframe writing assessment, and this strategic action includes several components, such as alliance building and communicating with others. In essence, we need to share our stories with all vested constituencies if we are going to succeed in reframing.

We build on these strategies in chapter five, "Reframing in Action," by moving from theoretical discussions of strategy to their real-world enactment. In this chapter we present five examples of writing assessments—in two- and four-year institutions, in writing programs and a writing center—that show the strategies and techniques in action and the give-and-take that occurs in practice.

After these case studies, we move beyond the institution in chapter six, "Reframing Writing Assessment: Why Does My Participation Matter?" Drawing on interviews with academic professionals (as well as our own experiences in these types of activities) representing a wide range of writing assessments that extend beyond the institution, we again focus on strategies and techniques for engaging in these important debates and discussions.

Chapter seven, "Re-imagining Writing Assessments," concludes the book. Here, we use the analysis developed throughout the book to offer a number of concrete, pragmatic, and ideally useful strategies that writing instructors, program directors, English department chairs, or other writing professionals can use in efforts to reframe writing assessment in their local contexts, and possibly—hopefully—beyond.

In the end, then, *Reframing Writing Assessment* is intended to offer a theoretical framework, concrete illustrations, and suggestions for action for all of us who care deeply and are invested in postsecondary writing instruction. As veterans of this work, we know it can be challenging in the best and most difficult ways. But we also believe that if we are to continue contributing to the ways students' educations are shaped—and, therefore, to what we can do in the classroom—it is some of the most important work that we do.

2

FRAMING (AND) AMERICAN EDUCATION

In chapter one, we suggested that postsecondary writing instruction and writing assessment orbits are at the center of a very large galaxy that includes questions about the purpose of a college education, expectations of "productive" citizens, and, ultimately, the nation's successful progress.

From documents like *Ready or Not*, an influential report published by the American Diploma Project (Achieve 2004), memos published by or in association with the Voluntary System of Accountability (e.g., McPherson and Shulenberger 2006), and other policy reports, it's possible to piece together a dominant narrative about the exigency surrounding these discussions about education. The problem, this story says, is that students aren't learning what they need to in order to *be* successful twenty-first- century citizens in postsecondary (or secondary) education. This story is so consistently repeated, in fact, that its components are interchangeable. "Three hundred and seventy years after the first college in our fledgling nation was established," begins *A Test of Leadership*, the report from the Spellings Commission, "higher education in the United States has become one of our greatest success stories" (Miller 2006, ix). "But even as we bask in the afterglow of past achievements," says *Accountability for Better Results*, a study published by the National Commission on Accountability in Higher Education (affiliated with the State Higher Education Executive Officers), "a starker reality is emerging on the horizon" (State Higher Education 2005, 6). "Where the United States was once the international leader in granting college degrees," notes *Ready to Assemble: Grading State Higher Education Accountability Systems*, "we've now fallen to 10th" (Adelman and Carey 2009, 1). "Significant reform is needed in education, worldwide, to respond to and shape global trends in support of both economic and social development," contends *Transforming Education,* a collaboration among Cisco, Intel, and Microsoft (Partners 2009, 1). "Our nation must become more educated to thrive and prosper in the knowledge economy of the twenty-first century," argues Paul Lingenfelter (2007, v).

In these reports and the many others like them, "the twenty-first-century economy," or "the knowledge economy," or "the twenty-first-century workforce" figures prominently, often coupled with the suggestion that school must prepare students for twenty-first-century jobs and/or careers. In some ways, these references are understandable. Until recently, the United States was seen as the world's economic powerhouse. As we live through the current economic downturn, we understand the real-time implications when workers are not hired and businesses large and small fail. In an analysis of the economic theories playing out in discussions about the nation's economic woes, Paul Krugman notes that "U.S. households have seen $13 trillion in wealth evaporate. More than six million jobs have been lost, and the unemployment rate appears headed for its highest level since 1940" (2009). Implied in this dominant story, situated within the specific context of the nation's economic crisis and the broader context of the need for school to prepare students for citizenship that we described briefly in chapter one, is that education should do something—fast—to help American households regain that wealth.

As understandable as this link between education and work is, though, it's not the *only* way "the purpose of education" can be conceptualized. Mike Rose, like others before him who have questioned the "commonsense" purposes presented for education (e.g., Noddings 2005) implores, "Think of what we don't read and hear" (Rose 2009, 27). Throughout this chapter and this book, we will return to "what we don't read and hear," but we first must examine what we *do* experience. In fact, the stories about education that run through reports like these (as well as news stories, and talk radio and other venues) are shaped through one (very, very dominant) *frame* currently surrounding the idea of "what education should be," a frame that also profoundly influences discussions about assessments intended to provide information about what students are learning as well as how and why they are learning it.

An important step in reframing writing assessment, then, is to understand the roots of this dominant frame and the ways it shapes contemporary representations of (writing) education. But before we can discuss the current frame, it's important to understand the concept of framing and how this concept is at work in current discussions about education. Learning about how framing (and reframing) operates can be crucial to our work as college writing instructors or program directors.

FRAMING: MAKING WINDOWS ON THE WORLD

In the analysis of the economic meltdown of the early twenty-first century that we quote from above, Paul Krugman (2009) argues that widespread participation in a common understanding of the economy contributed to economic collapse. Economists, he said, believed "that markets were inherently stable—indeed, that stocks and other assets were always priced just right." Rather than discuss whether or not this was in fact really the case, Krugman says that the "main division" among macroeconomists "was between those who insisted that free-market economies never go astray and those who believed that economies may stray now and then but that any major deviations from the path of prosperity could and would be corrected by the all-powerful Fed. But "neither side," he asserts, "was prepared to cope with an economy that went off the rails despite the Fed's best efforts."

Krugman's analysis points to how one perspective dominated economists' thinking about the economy through the twentieth century. In that sense, it is an illustration of a *frame*, a perspective that shapes understandings of situations or circumstances.

Lee Bolman, a business scholar, and Terence Deal, an education researcher, explain that frames are like "windows, maps, tools, lenses, orientations, [or] perspectives"—they shape an individual's or a group's perceptions of what is and is not plausible/ in the picture/focused/visible (2003, 12). Readers more familiar with theorists such as Kenneth Burke may see framing akin to Burke's argument that language and terminology affect the nature of our observations and understanding of reality, what Burke (1966) referred to as "terministic screens."

Perhaps the most effective way to consider the importance of a *frame* (an object) and *framing* as a process (an activity) is to think about the frame of a house. The frame constitutes the inner structure—the sort of skeleton—of the outer structure. The frame supports and eventually dictates what can be included as a part of the house. For example, if a builder wanted to construct an addition to the house, then he would have to build another frame for that section, but it would have to be linked to the original frame structurally. How the new and old frames are connected would be determined, in part, by the specifics of the addition. If the addition is a second story, then a new frame would be needed for it, but the original frame would also have to be reinforced or altered to withstand the added weight. In this sense, a frame is a noun, a thing. But *framing* is also a process—what a builder does to construct the skeleton of the house.

In the same way, the ideas of *frames* and *framing* can be applied to the constructions of what individuals and groups perceive to be realistic and feasible, or unrealistic and out of the realm of possibility. These perceptions, like the structure of a house, hang on individuals' understandings of their worlds, especially as they are reflected in and through communication. Wooden beams or other building materials are used to build the frame of a physical structure; language—written, verbal, signed, mathematical, or otherwise—is the only medium that humans have to represent how they understand and construct the interior structures around which their understandings of "reality" are formed. Thus, in Krugman's analysis, economists used mathematical formulae (a form of language) to construct and build on a model that "explained" economic growth (and explained away moments when growth did not occur).

The process of framing, similarly, shapes the ways that humans develop the skeletons of understandings upon which we then hang our understandings of people, situations, and the world(s) around us. The frames enable us to make and tell stories, establishing relationships between people and events: X is this way because Y, or Z is not this way because C. Using Krugman's example, we could say the economy (X) is robust because free market economies do not stray or, if they do, their divergences from progress can be corrected by the Federal Reserve (Y); the economy (Z) is not being constructed on a basis that involves the development and use of fictitious vehicles for financial transactions (e.g., derivatives, mark-to-market accounting, and so on) (C) because the free market economy does not stray in this way. Frames are strengthened, say communication researchers James Hertog and Douglas McLeod (2001), when they connect to stories shaped by the same frames. Krugman says economists, for example, built on a frame of "how the economy works" that was constructed as the nation recovered from the Great Depression, a frame that put enormous faith in the rationality and agency of markets. Relatively consistent growth from the 1950s through the 1990s reinforced the premises of this frame, and much of the economic work produced during this almost fifty-year stretch contributed to the perception of its stability. Even the decline of the stock market in 1973 and 1974 and the 1987 crash of the Dow were seen as "blips" from which the economy quickly recovered. The strength of the model— of the frame—was continually reinforced by a "great deal of statistical evidence, which at first seemed strongly supportive" (Krugman 2009).

But the economic collapse of the early twenty-first century quickly revealed a problem with the frame through which economists (and citizens) had viewed the economy, and with the activities through which they contributed to this ongoing process *of* framing. Because this frame was so dominant, economists weren't seeing other possibilities, other stories about what constituted the foundation (or lack thereof) of America's economic growth, outside of the frame. "The economics profession went astray," Krugman says, "because economists, as a group, mistook beauty, clad in impressive-looking mathematics, for truth. . . . [T]his romanticized and sanitized vision of the economy led most economists to ignore all the things that can go wrong" (2009). He concludes his analysis by suggesting that economists need to adopt a different theoretical perspective than the one that has dominated economic work through much of the twentieth century and incorporate more contact with actual financial transactions (rather than just macroeconomic analysis) into their work. "Many economists," he says, "will find these changes deeply disturbing."

As Krugman's analysis illustrates, it's often easiest to see (and take apart) frames and the process through which they have been constructed when the structures they support become destabilized, just as it is easy to see the frame of a house before it's built or when it is being torn down. When structures exist and are standing, though, those frames are far harder to recognize because they're covered. This is even more the case when the frames are ideological, not physical, as is the case with education. When frames become established and are built upon by additional stories and additional examples, the ideas they support become "common sense." Antonio Gramsci (1985) used the term *hegemony* to refer to the dominant ideology that is formed when a loose, informal, but networked association of concepts cluster together and form a sense of "reality" through dominant frames. Raymond Williams, building on Gramsci, notes that this association is a process and a system that "constitutes a[n absolute] sense of reality for most people . . . beyond which it is very difficult for most members of the society to move, in most areas of their lives" (1973, 5). Thus, we return to Mike Rose's point. "For a long time now," he says, "our public talk about education has been shaped by a concern about economic readiness and competitiveness" (2009, 25). But even this discussion, of course, is framed to include and exclude particular perspectives—about inequities in school funding, about the disappearance of the "social safety net" (27). Instead, the idea that "education should prepare students for college and career" is seen as a commonsense purpose of school.

FRAMING (WRITING) EDUCATION

The process of framing, then, results in the construction of ideological structures that shape understandings of how things work, why things are as they are, and what should happen based on that status. Understanding this process and the frames that are built (and added to) as a result of it is an important step in reframing writing assessment. The next step is forming an understanding of the current frame surrounding writing education and assessment, and learning about the issues that emerge from that existing frame. This step is akin to taking a look at the frame that lies underneath the very large, strongly built house in which we currently live.[1]

The Sub-basement: A Bit on Education and the Nation's Progress

Krugman's analysis of the economy examines foundational theories about the market upon which our economy is constructed. In the same way, ideas about the relationship between education and "the nation's future" form the sub-basement of the framework upon which contemporary conceptions of education are built. Just as in Krugman's analysis, it is possible— at a certain level of abstraction—to identify broad similarities between these ideas. For instance, the idea that "school should prepare students to be productive citizens" is a statement that could apply equally across almost all theories of learning and schooling. These theories, similarly, fall under some broader

---

1. Of course, we acknowledge that our analysis of the process of framing and of frames currently underscoring education *also* reflects perspectives on the process of framing and of education—so the same analysis we are undertaking here could be done to our work, as well.

ideas about what is necessary for the nation's progress; while there is also disagreement among those theories (e.g., what "progress" means, what is necessary to achieve it), there is general agreement among them that the idea *of* progress is generally a good one.

But since the beginning of the common school movement in the United States, there has not been widespread consensus—even among educators—beyond a very general level of abstraction about what students should learn and how those things should be taught.[2] Curriculum historian William H. Schubert describes a tension between "two opposing notions of science" underscoring this debate: "The social behaviorist seeks inquiry that controls others through highly generalized knowledge derived by credentialed experts, and the experimentalist searches with others for insights about the consequences of daily courses of action on growth for all involved" (1986, 77). The issues have revolved around some key questions: What does it mean to be a productive citizen? And how should education cultivate productivity based on this definition?

Historians have examined ideas about "productive citizenship" in the nineteenth and twentieth centuries, and how schooling could or should contribute to the development of this kind of citizen. Independently of each other, Warren Susman (1984) and David Tyack (2003) have outlined two definitions of these citizens and the role that education should take in creating them. From what Susman (1984) calls a "stewardly" perspective and Tyack (2003) a "humanitarian" one, the assumption is that productive citizens are those who contribute to the growth of the democracy, and that all citizens have the capacity to make this contribution. School, as a social institution dedicated to this growth, should cultivate students' innate, natural inclinations to be productive citizens by tapping into their natural interests and helping them understand the connections

---

2. As curriculum historian Schubert (1986) demonstrates, it is possible to extend this argument back to education's development through the Greek and Roman Empire, the Renaissance, the Enlightenment, and so on, as well.

between those interests and the nation's broader goals. From the other perspective, which Susman (1984) calls "technocratic" and Tyack (2003) "interventionist," the presumption is that productive citizens are those who fulfill particular roles identified for them (by managers), and these roles are predetermined to contribute to the nation's progress in particular ways. In school, students' abilities are identified, and then learners can be sorted into different groups in order to have these abilities cultivated appropriately. While some students are destined for leadership, others are meant to follow; the job of education is to discover and shape leaders and followers.

David Labaree (1997), meanwhile, has identified three *purposes of schooling* associated with creating productive citizens that pervade the nineteenth and twentieth centuries. These purposes place the perspectives on citizenship identified by Susman (1984) and Tyack (2003) into an even broader context of the American economy and questions about whether education is seen a *public good* or a *private* one. The first purpose of schooling identified by Labaree, which he labels "democratic equality," contends that education is ultimately a public good. In order for the nation to succeed, its youth must be "prepare[d] . . . with equal care to take on the full responsibilities of citizenship in a competent manner" (1997, 42). The second purpose, which Labaree calls "social efficiency," also contends that education is a public good. But where the emphasis in "democratic equality" is on civic participation, this second model posits that the nation's "well-being depends on our ability to prepare the young to carry out useful economic roles with competence" (42). The third purpose, finally, positions education as a private good. In this purpose, which Labaree calls "social mobility, . . . education is a commodity, the only purpose of which is to provide individual students with a competitive advantage in the struggle for desirable social positions. The aim is to get more of this valuable commodity than one's competitors" (42).

Labaree's analysis of the three purposes that education might serve provides an overarching concept surrounding Tyack's and Susman's. The question raised by his purposes of school is whether the nation's growth will be aided by *collective gain*, as in the democratic equality and social efficiency models, or *individual gain*, as in the social mobility model. This raises a subsequent question about how stewardly and technocractic conceptions of citizenship and education interact with these ideas about growth. For instance, if progress is to be achieved when citizens are equipped to contribute to the democratic polis, education could proceed from the presumption that the role of education (and teachers) is to help students find their ways into particular roles. Alternatively, it could proceed from the presumption that education should identify the roles best suited to students and groom them for these roles. Similarly, if progress is to be achieved when citizens are equipped to contribute to the nation's economic well-being, education could help students find the best economic fits, or identify those fits and educate students for them. Both of these models are predicated on the idea that education is a public good that should help students contribute to collective gain, and that the nation's progress is dependent on this shared effort. On the other hand, education could be predicated on the idea that progress is achieved through the competition of one individual against another and the amassing of social and intellectual capital. In this case, the stewardly (or humanitarian) approach to education isn't especially appropriate; instead, education is a private good that presumes individuals have or can be led to cultivate particular abilities, but the goal in honing those abilities is individual advancement.

These ideas about "productive citizenship" and the role that education should play in preparing citizens to contribute to the nation's forward movement, then, constitute the sub-basement of the frames upon which American education is constructed. But the issue, as this analysis suggests, is that there are multiple and sometimes conflicting ideas here. Of course, as noted earlier, it is possible to achieve a level of abstraction that will accommodate all of these ideas as well, thus obviating any differences

between them. For the purposes of *reframing*, both these differences and this larger level of abstraction are potentially useful,
an issue to which we will return in chapters three and four.

The First Floor: Education and the Twenty-First-Century Economy

Susman's, Tyack's, and Labaree's discussions of ideas about
citizenship and education are based on analyses of nineteenth-
and twentieth-century processes. A sharper focus on the twenty-
first century provides a more clearly defined picture of the current frame surrounding discussions about education—the sort
of first floor of the building where we currently live—and the
ways that conceptions of citizenship and education identified by
these researchers play out in the new millennium.

Even before the economic meltdown of late 2008, there was
a sense that individual advancement of the kind outlined by
Labaree (1997), a sense of personal social mobility that has reso-
nated in American culture since the Horatio Alger stories of the
early twentieth century, would not be enough. What would be
required, instead, was a collective *social* emphasis on the kind of
individuation, tracking, and fulfillment of economic need that
was previously associated primarily with individual achievement.
Rather than creating structures, including educational systems,
where individuals would have the opportunity to cultivate *their
own* potential for *individual* benefit, in the current frame it is
the responsibility of the system itself to cultivate individuals'
economic potential because the *nation's* economic well-being is
dependent on the ability of these individuals to reach that potential. Evidence of this shift can be easily located in the debate over
education funding included in the 2009 federal stimulus bill.
One of the compromises in the draft bill shifted a portion of
roughly $81 billion in proposed support for educational institu-
tions and infrastructures to $13.9 billion in Pell grants awarded
to individual students with economic need (Lederman, 2009).[3]

---

3. The proposed fiscal year 2011 budget, which includes major changes to the
   Elementary and Secondary Reauthorization Act, also includes a hefty alloca-
   tion for Pell Grants, as well as a proposal that Pell grant funding be moved

In other words, it shifted money from support for the *educational system* to support for *individual students within the system*, but not the system itself. This means that while more students might have support to attend college, the systemic and structural issues associated with colleges (from inadequate instructional staff, to understaffed support programs, to deferred maintenance on facilities) would not be addressed.

This emphasis on *individual success* as the keystone for *collective success* is also evident in assessment questions that use aggregated data on individual students to determine the collective performance of a system (such as a local public school district) or an educational institution (such as a community college or a comprehensive university). The Elementary and Secondary Reauthorization Act of 2001, better known as No Child Left Behind (NCLB), called for just this: all students would be tested; schools, districts, and states would be evaluated by students' performance on assessments. This approach is in contrast to one in which a sample of students is tested and the performance of the district or state is inferred from the performance of the sample, as in the National Assessment of Educational Progress (NAEP), published by the National Center for Educational Studies, which tests only a sample of students and does not report individual scores of students or even schools. (There are other significance differences between NCLB and NAEP, but those are beyond our interests here.) In this perspective, then, education's role as a public good—and the nation's progress— is related to its ability to cultivate an individual's *private* gain.

The patchwork of quotes from contemporary policy reports discussed earlier in this chapter illustrates the exigency created through this framework. The story that emerges from this amalgam of excerpts says education should prepare students for the twenty-first century economy, but that schools and teachers don't really understand what is necessary to achieve this preparation. As a result, this story says, students are arriving in college

---

from discretionary to mandatory status (Klein 2011).

and in workplaces after college underprepared. Colleges and universities are then forced to provide "remedial" education, costing taxpayers millions of dollars. Perhaps more importantly, the skills students lack upon entering and leaving college are preventing them from achieving the individual success upon which the democracy depends. As the framework surrounding this story becomes stronger (through its repetition in policy documents, news stories, everyday conversations, and so on), the questions emerging from it revolve not around *whether* it is appropriate—might there not be other ways to conceive of the purpose(s) of school?—but *how* to achieve the purpose outlined in this framework. Additionally, implied in this story is a critique of the stewardly approach that suggests development should build upon students' existing knowledge, cultivated by expert teachers who understand (through their training) how to nurture students into the democracy. This is replaced by a technocratic approach that focuses on the development and demonstration of learning outcomes expressed as "standards."

ADVANCING THE FRAME: A TEST OF LEADERSHIP, ACCREDITATION, AND ASSESSMENT

A Test of Leadership, the final report from the Spellings Commission on the Future of Higher Education, provides a vivid illustration of how this tight frame surrounds and perpetuates particular stories about postsecondary education (Miller et al. 2006). Issued in 2006, the critiques in the report have been seized upon by postsecondary institutions and organizations alike as they attempt to grapple with the question of what a college or university education should be and do in the twenty-first century United States. *A Test of Leadership* extended the "crisis" frame used in reports like *A Nation at Risk* (U. S. Department of Ed.), the 1983 report proclaiming that "'a rising tide of mediocrity'" in K–12 education was putting America at an economic disadvantage in global competition, to post-secondary education. To see this document as separating school's historical purpose of citizenship cultivation from the notion of preparing citizens (e.g., Green 2009), though, is to lose sight of the conflicting definitions of citizenship described by Labaree (1997) and others. In fact, *A Test of Leadership* forges a strong bond between individuals' economic successes and the nation's forward progress.

A Test of Leadership, also referred to as the Spellings Report, opens with the story that the purpose of education is to prepare students for democracy, but that postsecondary educators no longer understand the shape of that democracy. Thus, the report says, educators and institutions must either retool, or run the risk of surrendering the agency that enables them to prepare students through education. This position is outlined in two paragraphs early in the document. The first reaffirms the "preparation" frame:

> U.S. higher education institutions must recommit themselves to their core public purposes. For close to a century now, access to higher education has been a principle—some would say the principle—means of achieving social mobility. Much of our nation's inventiveness has been centered in colleges and universities, as has our commitment to a kind of democracy that only an educated and informed citizenry makes possible. (Miller et al. 2006, ix)

The second establishes the extent to which post-secondary education no longer understands the nature of twenty-first-century democracy:

> But today that world is becoming tougher, more competitive, less forgiving of wasted resources and squandered opportunities. In tomorrow's world a nation's wealth will derive from its capacity to educate, attract, and retain citizens who are able to work smarter and learn faster—making educational achievement even more important both for individuals and society writ large. (Miller et al. 2006, ix)

The report then goes on to identify three key areas in which the "crisis" in higher education is most acute: access (to higher learning by all Americans), affordability (costs, including the process of applying for financial aid), and accountability. In this latter area, it raises red flags around what students are learning, how, and why. It proclaims:

> Despite increased attention to student learning by colleges and universities and accreditation agencies, parents and students have no solid evidence, comparable across institutions, of how much students learn in colleges or whether they learn more at one college than at another. Similarly, policymakers need more comprehensive data to help them decide whether the national investment in higher education is paying off and how taxpayer dollars could be used more effectively. (Miller et al. 2006, 13)

The report contends that colleges and universities should use data to "stimulate innovation and continuous improvement" (Miller at al. 2006, 14) but that, traditionally, the data collected did not provide adequate information about what students were learning.

The Spellings Report, Postsecondary Assessment, and Institutional Accreditation

The Spellings Report focuses particular attention on the process by which postsecondary institutions are accredited, which it says "has significant shortcomings" (Miller et al. 2006, 14). It is in the discussion of the problems with postsecondary assessment and the implications for postsecondary accreditation that the report most clearly reflects the dominant frame-shaping stories about education that we have described here. To understand how this is, though, it is important to spend a bit of time outlining the relationship between postsecondary institutions and the U.S. Department of Education. While we may not hear these discussions directly in our positions as classroom teachers or program directors, readers can bet someone on their campus—an assessment director, a provost, a president—is considering the issues that swirl around in them.

Within the structure of postsecondary education, the federal government can exercise only indirect power. That is because postsecondary institutions report not to the Department of

Education (as K–12 institutions do, often through their state's departments of education), but to accrediting agencies. There are seven major regional accrediting bodies in the United States and one national agency, the Council on Higher Education Accreditation (CHEA). There are also countless specialized accreditors, such as the Association of Advanced Rabbinical and Talmudic Schools Accrediting Commission. For institutions to receive federal funding, and for their students to be eligible for federal financial aid, they must be accredited by one of these bodies. This relationship is outlined in figure 1.

Accrediting agencies do not set standards; instead, accreditors ensure that *institutions* are setting standards, assessing how and whether those standards are being achieved, and constantly working to improve teaching and learning within those standards. Accreditors are invested with the authority to undertake this work by the Department of Education, which traditionally has been guided by the National Advisory Committee on Institutional Quality and Integrity (NACIQI), intended to be a bipartisan committee whose members are appointed by Congress. Accreditors and the U.S. Department of Education regularly negotiate a set of rules that guide their work and the relationships to one another, a process known as negotiated rule making.[4]

But the Spellings Report claims that the accreditation process "has significant shortcomings" (Miller et al. 2006, 14), and that postsecondary institutions had not, as of 2006, "embraced opportunities for innovation" (15). Thus, the report recommends that "higher education . . . change from a system based

---

4. In addition to national accrediting bodies, many academic departments participate in discipline-specific accreditation processes such as the National Council for Accreditation of Teacher Education (NCATE), the Teacher Education Accreditation Council (TEAC), or the Accreditation Board for Engineering and Technology (ABET). These accrediting bodies are sometimes also members of CHEA. Some states require colleges and universities to participate in discipline-specific assessments, as well; for example, in Michigan, departments and colleges of education are required to be certified by NCATE or TEAC. These specialized accreditors do set standards and guidelines for certification, and sometimes also establish assessment processes.

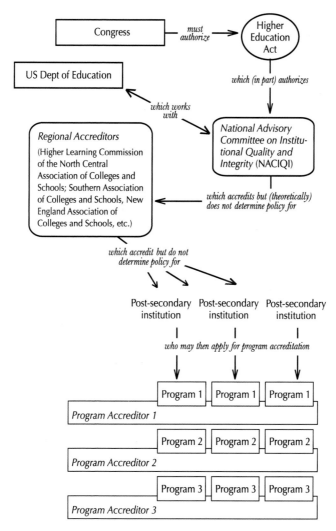

Fig. 1. DOE/Educational Institution Relationship

primarily on reputation to one based on performance" and "urges the creation of a robust culture of accountability and transparency throughout higher education. Every one of our goals," the report says, "will be more easily achieved if higher education embraces and implements serious accountability measures" (20).

Some of these include:

- aligning secondary and postsecondary standards (17);
- developing "initiatives that help states hold high schools accountable for teaching all students" (18);
- calling for postsecondary institutions to "improve institutional cost management through the development of new performance benchmarks designed to measure and improve productivity and efficiency" and develop "measures" that would enable "consumers and policymakers to see institutional results in the areas of academic quality, productivity, and efficiency" (20);
- shifting from "a system primarily based on reputation to one based on performance" (20);
- developing and using assessment mechanisms that could "measure student learning using quality-assessment data" (24);
- making publicly available the results of "student learning assessments, including value-added measurements . . . indicat[ing] how students' skills have improved over time" (24); and
- calling for accrediting agencies to develop frameworks that "align—and expand—existing accreditation standards" to "allow comparison among institutions regarding learning outcomes and other performance measures; encourage innovation and continuous improvement; and require institutions and programs to move toward world-class quality relative to specific missions and report measurable progress in relationship to their national and international peers" (25).[5]

---

5. See Huot (2007), Adler-Kassner (2008), and Green (2009) for responses to the Spelling Commission's report from the perspective of composition specialists.

In recommending processes that allude to standardization of assessment (and, perhaps, of learning), these recommendations reflect the dominant frame-shaping stories about education in crisis and contribute to the development of an educational system that prepares students for participation in a technocratic economy. But because of the foundations upon which that education process is based, the recommendations also indirectly address conceptions of education and citizenship embedded in the guidelines shaping postsecondary education and accreditation. These conceptions (which are themselves rooted in late nineteenth and early twentieth-century ideas about education and the development of the modern-day academy, as we will discuss in chapters three and four) rely on the idea that postsecondary educators, experts in their fields, understand the particular kinds of citizenship to which their disciplines are best suited, and how the knowledge of their disciplines should be communicated to students in order to suit students for those citizenly roles. It is for educators, then, to determine what is important for students to learn, to invoke their expertise to assess whether those determinations are appropriate, and to ascertain whether and how the methods by which these instructional goals (and assessments) are being accomplished are effective (see Bender 1993). This is the basis for the system of peer review used by regional accreditors (and many others)—as well as the basis for the formation of academic disciplines and departments in their most traditional forms.

In raising questions about and possibilities for accreditation, then, the Spellings Report simultaneously addresses accreditors and the system of faculty authority and expertise upon which contemporary postsecondary education rests. The report hints strongly that accreditors should either establish (or force institutions to establish) common standards and then ensure that institutions are achieving these standards, thereby circumventing the authority of disciplinary experts and undermining the peer review system upon which accreditation (and, in fact, the entire academy) has been based. For this reason, many believed the recommendations in *A Test of Leadership* would radically alter the relationship between postsecondary institutions and accrediting agencies, which have never *set* standards, but rather have ensured that institutions are setting and assessing learning goals.

Ultimately, for a variety of reasons outside the scope of this discussion, the process of negotiated rule making by which the Department of Education hoped to mandate some of these recommendations in 2006–2007 failed. However, in mid–2008 the Higher Education Act (HEA) was reauthorized. The revision of the act includes some measures that take into account the Spellings Report's attempt to move institutions toward standardized learning goals. These include the following provisions:

- Postsecondary institutions to "set[] [their] own specific standards and measures [of student learning] consistent with . . . [their] mission[s] and within the larger framework of the accreditation standards";

- Institutions, "in consultation . . . with accreditors," to "set common standards used to review all of the institutions they accredit"; and

- Accreditors to apply standards to institutions "that respect the stated missions of institutions" (American Council on Education 2008, 2–3).

In the final analysis, then, the HEA—which outlines the relationship between the Department of Education and the accreditors who ultimately do have authority over postsecondary institutions—does not call the imposed standards included in the early drafts of the Spellings Report, or even the calls for "alignment" and uniform standards in the official document. However, it does call for accreditors to ensure that institutions are establishing learning outcomes consistent with the institution's missions.

(WRITING)ASSESSMENT: PURPOSES AND AUDIENCES

The recommendations outlined in *A Test of Leadership*, particularly the suggestions about the idea of set end points, provoked strong reactions among postsecondary instructors, administrators, and accreditors. Through its push for greater "accountability," couched within recommendations about assessment like those described above, many perceived it as a push for a fundamental shift in the role that the federal government could play in assessment. Then-President of the Higher Learning Commission (HLC) Steve Crow, for instance, said that discussions of accreditation had long swung between an emphasis on "performance accountability" and "a focus on students' learning" (2007, 2). But the Spellings Report, he said, represents a new take on the accountability emphasis. This time, he said, "the term 'accountability' is linked directly to the achievement of . . . broad national goals" (4). As such, it

> share[s] a specific view about the purpose of higher education in the United States. Namely, that in this global economy, this newly flattened world, the U.S. is highly reliant on its colleges and universities to ensure that the nation is not only highly competitive but continues to be the recognized global leader in most aspects of the knowledge economy. [The report] therefore focus[es] on how colleges and universities must provide the nation with both sufficient and necessary intellectual capacity by providing the learning required by a high level workforce in a high tech global economy. (Crow 2007, 4)

Given this, Crow asked, "[W]here does assessment of student learning, as we have come to love it, fit into this definition of accountability? . . . It is not lost on me that in many institutions faculty and administrators begin to understand the power of creating a culture of evidence better when they wrestle with a concrete issue rather measure themselves against accreditation standards" (2007, 6). Crow's response highlights the tension between locally based standards and assessments (within the context of institution, discipline, and faculty) and the idea of uniform, decontextualized standards.

The differences between the report's recommendations and Crow's discussion of assessment also point to two significant questions that, four years after the appearance of the Spellings Report, remain vital for educators to consider in the process of reframing writing assessment: What purpose does and should assessment serve? And who should be served by assessment? The typical response at the postsecondary level has been class-room teachers, programs, and/or institutions, as the assessment literature in composition attests. In a review of approaches to assessment, for instance, Kathleen Blake Yancey (1999) identi-fies three waves of writing assessment through the mid- and late twentieth century. Despite differences in conceptualizations of writing, the location of disciplinary expertise, and appropriate assessment methodology, all imply that assessment was to be used for internal purposes—to inform decisions about which writing classes students should take first, or to help instructors in a writing program understand how students are doing and make changes based on writing performance (Yancey 1999).

But the Spellings Report suggests that internally-focused assessment isn't enough. Instead, like many other documents that reflect the same crisis-oriented story that frames it, *A Test of Leadership* wavers between a call for processes that will "prove" what is or is not happening in the classroom for an audience of *public* stakeholders—taxpayers, employers, and parents—and occasional calls for classroom instructors to use assessment to improve their own work. In one of the early critiques of the report, Brian Huot (2007) comments on this inconsistency, not-ing that on the one hand, the report calls for "the creation of 'outcomes based accountability systems designed to be accessi-ble and useful for students, policymakers, and the public as well as for internal management and institutional improvement'", and on the other "not[ing] that '[f]aculty must be at the forefront of defining educational objectives for students and developing meaningful, evidence-based measures of progress toward those goals'" (qtd. in Huot , 519). Huot goes on to comment that "this seem[s] to be in direct opposition to the other accountability measures [described in the report]" (519).

While compositionists like Huot (2007) have done important work in pointing out this inconsistency (as well as many other problematic issues in the report), grappling with the questions about purpose(s) and audience(s) is perhaps the most significant challenge that writing instructors and program directors (as well as other postsecondary educators) face with regard to reframing writing assessment. The challenge involves understanding and honoring conceptualizations of learning, development, and writing that might be quite different from our own, while simultaneously attempting to make connections between these different conceptions and research-based best practices. The risk that we face in *not* resolving this issue is considerable, as our K–12 colleagues can attest. For the last fifteen or so years, especially, they have contended in various ways with mandated assessments designed to speak to purposes and audiences often outside their control. Countless teachers tell stories about the ways in which they are forced to teach to tests so that they, their districts, and their students can "prove" they are doing what they are told needs to be done in the classroom (e.g., Callahan 1997; Hillocks 2002; and O'Neill et al. 2005). Daryl Szymanski, a high school teacher in southeastern Michigan, vividly describes the problems that emerge for teachers because of these constraints:

> The pressure to teach to both the content and assessment practices of the ACT [which, in Michigan, is used as the Michigan Education Assessment Program test for high school juniors] results in the burden of striking a balance between spending too much time teaching to the test and providing meaningful and authentic learning experiences. Specifically, in the area of writing, too much time is spent on one format, the genre of writing that is required of the assessment. For the ACT Writing Assessment—the assessment used in Michigan—the format is a 30-minute, in-class assessment, and the genre is a persuasive essay. In [my district], this has become the

preferred genre for required high school English classes. Of the
nine district-mandated writing assessments that are required over
the course of a year, five mimic the ACT Writing Assessment, and
the remaining four are literature-based essays that are aligned with
the literary units of study for each course for each quarter. (2009, 2)

Assessment scholar David Shupe (2008) has defined more
clearly the issues surrounding the multiple purposes of and
audiences for assessment. First, Shupe identifies four distinct purposes that assessment is expected to serve. It should
provide individual students with a "record of . . . cumulative
results"; keep track of student learning and, ideally, help students to improve learning; demonstrate overall improvement
of educational results within the institution; and provide an
overall record of educational results. Additionally, assessment
is expected to demonstrate institutions' work with these four
purposes to internal and external audiences (2008, 72–73).
Lynn Priddy (2009), Vice President for Assessment at the
Higher Learning Commission, has built upon Shupe's analysis
in a matrix that demonstrates these multiple purposes (see also
Adler-Kassner and Harrington n.d.).

Shupe's and Priddy's analyses can provide a framework to
situate existing assessment work and to identify areas of need
with regard to the important questions about purposes of and
audiences for assessment described above. In composition and
rhetoric, for instance, we have focused almost exclusively on
conducting student and program-based assessments whose goals
are to *improve student learning* for internal audiences—members
of our programs or, in some instances, others within our institutions represented by the left side of the matrix in figure 2.
We also have raised questions about how the idea of "effective
application of learning" included in the lower right quadrant
of the matrix is defined. We have argued strongly that literacy
practices are local and contextual, and that evidence of effective
learning lies in the ability to adapt and continue to learn, rather
than to immediately manifest skills required in specific situations

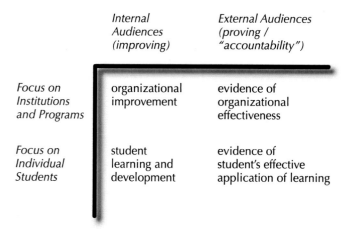

	Internal Audiences (improving)	External Audiences (proving / "accountability")
Focus on Institutions and Programs	organizational improvement	evidence of organizational effectiveness
Focus on Individual Students	student learning and development	evidence of student's effective application of learning

Fig. 2. Assessment Purposes Matrix

and/or workplaces. (See, for instance, the Conference on College Composition and Communication [CCCC] Statement on Assessment [2006] or the National Council of Teachers of English-Writing Program Administrators [NCTE-WPA] White Paper on Writing Assessment in Colleges and Universities [2008], both of which are based on research and research-based best practices in the field.) The flourishing literature on assessment attests to the acumen with which composition instructors can, by now, undertake *locally-based* assessments that reflect principles and practices recognized as valid both within the educational assessment literature, and within the principles outlined by our own discipline (see, for instance, Broad 2003; Broad et al. 2009; Huot 2002; Lynne 2008; and O'Neill, Huot, and Moore 2009 for some of the most frequently cited examples of this work).

But as important as the questions asked and efforts propelled by classroom and program assessment are—and we think that they are absolutely crucial—they do not yet effectively speak to questions about education and student learning asked by those *outside* the academy. These questions, about how or whether institutions can prove that (and/or to what extent) students are learning what they are supposed to, come from the upper right quadrant of the matrix: they are intended to compel institutions to *determine or demonstrate* (not improve) institutional effectiveness for audiences outside the academy. The Spellings Report provides one illustration of this; others can be located in documents connected with the Voluntary System of Accountability (e.g., McPherson and Shulenberger 2006), reports issued by Achieve and the American Diploma Project, or almost any other organization studying and/or advocating for particular issues in or approaches to postsecondary education. This is because, as we have suggested, the frame surrounding these discussions perpetuates and reinforces the idea that education (K–16) should prepare students to become active participants in the twenty-first- century economy, and there are doubts about whether that preparation is occurring successfully right now. Like other large-scale assessment efforts, these involve outlining the broadest boundaries—an entire college or university, even a cluster of institutions seen as "comparable" in some way—and then using large-scale assessments to determine whether the institution is effectively achieving outcomes determined (often by the creators of the assessments, who typically have advisory boards or other processes for input) to be important for all students within the defined boundaries. And while we might not agree with the frame (for learning, citizenship, participation, or other values) these current questions reflect, we must recognize that they are entirely legitimate—that, in fact, publics outside the academy should understand what is happening in postsecondary classes and institutions.

Communicating with those outside of our programs, disciplines, and institutions who have concerns about institutional performance (as it is indicated in student work), we contend, is the most vexing challenge writing directors and instructors face in our efforts to reframe writing assessment. To restate: there is a very legitimate desire on the part of constituencies outside the academy (and the educational system more generally) to understand what is happening inside the system, and an equally legitimate need to understand how the work of this system is preparing students for some kind of future. How that future is defined, of course, is hugely important, as we note above, and helps to form the foundations for discussions about what education should do and how that doing should be assessed, by whom, how, and for what purposes. At the same time, there is a very legitimate desire on the part of on-the-ground instructors and program directors—people like the two of us and, very likely, many of you reading this book—to use assessment as a process to study the work of a writing classroom or program in order to find out what is happening in that program, and to use that research to improve that work. The problem, though, is that these purposes and audiences, at present, are held to be somewhat different from one another. The public discourse tends to focus around quantitative data that will *prove* what is (or is not) taking place in classrooms; the discourse in the profession tends to focus around qualitative data designed to help instructors *improve* the work of their classroom or program. While it might be tempting to see these two discussions as opposite ends of a spectrum, though, we return to the matrix in figure 2 (Priddy 2009). To reframe writing assessment, we must work to situate these efforts *in relation* to one another, rather than *in opposition* to one another. Developing strategies to approach this challenge is the subject of chapters four and five; in the next chapter, we situate writing assessment and higher education historically to provide more context in which to understand current frames surrounding both.

3

THE FRAMING OF COMPOSITION AND WRITING ASSESSMENT

In chapter two, we discussed how the current frame surrounding stories of American education perpetuates and builds upon existing tales of the purpose of school. This frame currently shapes a dominant story about postsecondary education focusing on "preparation for college and career," linking individual economic success to national progress. It has also led to a number of issues linked to the purposes and audiences for assessment that illustrate the differences that often exist between the many individuals and groups who are invested in postsecondary education, from instructors to future employers.

In this chapter, we examine the framing of topics and issues probably more familiar to most of us: composition and writing assessment. Within our discipline, as elsewhere, frames and framing often operate at an unconscious level, drawing on cultural values and creating structures for understanding reality, defining common sense, and producing cultural narratives. Just as reframing requires a broad understanding of these frames and the stories they produce about postsecondary education generally, so we must understand the stories that extend from the frames surrounding composition and writing assessment as well. These frames shape our perspectives just as they shape those of others. The early frames for the teaching, learning and assessing of writing—which in many ways conflict with those constructed by contemporary compositionists and literacy experts—continue to influence how composition and writing assessment are positioned in the academy as well as in contemporary conversations about written literacy. We begin by briefly reviewing the history of writing assessment to reveal the frames that surrounded English composition as a teaching subject when it was introduced into the college curriculum. From there, we examine the dominant values, theories, and practices that frame contemporary composition. We end this chapter by first exploring the implications of this disciplinary framework for writing assessment, and then secondly arguing that contemporary psychometric theory complements much of the writing assessment theory and practice that compositionists endorse.

Our aim in articulating the dominant frames used by composition specialists is to help writing teachers, administrators, and scholars make more conscious decisions about what values and positions we want to reinforce in our local contexts as well as in the larger community. Our goal—one we share with others such as Broad (2003), Haswell (2001), and Huot (2002)—is for writing scholars and teachers to be knowledgeable about writing assessment so we can harness the power associated both with the process of undertaking this research and with the idea of assessment itself to improve teaching and learning. However, we also want to change the way we talk about writing assessment within our field and beyond it. The language we use in discussions about this work—the ways we talk about it within our courses and programs, and the conversations we have with constituencies and stakeholders on and off campus—influences how writing assessment is understood and used by us and others. As we explained in the previous chapter and will discuss more extensively in the next, language helps to construct and reify frames humans use to understand and make sense of the worlds around us. Additionally, language influences the potential of the research we conduct under the mantle of assessment to improve teaching and learning. Because language is not neutral but always carries with it connotations and values, we as a field need to consciously consider the language we use in discussions about writing instruction and assessment. We need to understand how our language frames our work, and we need to make strategic, informed choices about our language and actions so that the frames we construct reinforce our values and support our aims. While we recognize that readers have their own individual values and beliefs (just as we as authors do), what we are articulating here are those values and assumptions the field of composition and rhetoric holds, as expressed in position statements (such as those published by the National Council of Teachers of English, the Conference on College Composition and Communication, and the Council of Writing Program Administrators) and scholarship (published in peer-reviewed journals, edited collections, and monographs).[1]

EXPOSING HISTORICAL FRAMES SURROUNDING COMPOSITION AND WRITING ASSESSMENT

Scholars have linked the history of composition as a course and a disciplinary field of study to classical rhetoric, which was the centerpiece of the college curriculum through the renaissance and into the eighteenth and nineteenth centuries.[2] However, the beginning of contemporary composition, characterized by a focus on the composition of original written discourse in English instead of the translation of Greek or Latin, is associated with the introduction of a required composition into the battery of entrance exams for Harvard students in 1874. This seemingly small curricular shift provides a concise and effective illustration of the connection between framing, assessment, and broader cultural and ideological goals. The purpose of the exam and instruction was to reform—and transform—both secondary and higher education.

In his attempt to make English the primary language of the college and the elective curriculum, Charles Eliot, President of

---

1. We realize that the composition and rhetoric community is not monolithic and that there are debates and discrepancies over many issues within the field. However, we see documents such as the policy briefs and summaries of research published by NCTE (available at http://www.ncte.org/policy-research) as representative of mainstream composition and rhetoric theories, practices, values, and beliefs.

2. In this historical overview, we draw on a variety of scholars who have written about the history of composition and rhetoric, most notably Brereton (1995), Connors (1997), Crowley (1998), Kitzhaber (1990), Horner (1990) and Douglas (1976), Elliot (2005), and O'Neill, Moore and Huot (2009).

Harvard at the time, sought to change Harvard from a finishing school for the sons of the elite class to a training facility for leaders of the emerging industrial economy, "a selection mechanism, a recruiting ground for new men for the apparatuses of state and industry, some few of whom might even come to walk the corridors of power themselves" (Douglas 2009, 95). This shift reflected changing patterns in American culture in the late nineteenth and early twentieth centuries, when the nation was moving away from an agrarian base toward an increasingly industrial one. Along with this shift came emphases on efficiency and professionalism, foci that seem to be incorporated in Eliot's emphasis on training professional employees. At the same time, many in the American elite were preoccupied with the transatlantic usage debates of the 1860s, when educated classes in the United States were "suddenly swept up in a wave of anxiety about the propriety of their speech and writing" (Connors 1997, 184). By the 1870s, there was much public outcry "bemoaning the 'illiteracy of American boys' and suggesting various solutions" with the most popular being "form-based mechanical lessons that came to be known as 'grammar'" (129). Educational institutions, including Harvard, responded to this anxiety. The emphasis on English composition, then, helped to establish stronger boundaries (and a stronger frame) around language and practices considered "acceptably" aligned with the values and ideologies associated with the burgeoning industrial economy of the late nineteenth and early twentieth centuries at the same time as it established differences between those practices and those considered "less acceptable."

The format of Harvard's entrance exams, typically impromptu essays based on a literary reading list, emphasized that preparation for college writing—and the assessment of it—should focus on timed, spontaneous writing that was not related to any particular context, but was presumed to be linked to skills that would be useful for a number of writing situations (see Brereton 1995 for examples of early exams). In keeping with the emphasis on "appropriate" language practices, the evaluation criteria privileged grammar, mechanics, and usage as well as references to the "right" kinds of literature. In 1879, Adams Sherman Hill, whom Eliot hired to administer the exam, teach composition, and run the program, reported in "An Answer to the Cry for More English":

> Those of us who have been doomed to read manuscripts written in an examination room—whether at a grammar school, a high school, or a college—have found the work of even good scholars disfigured by bad spelling, confusing punctuation, ungrammatical, obscure ambiguous, or inelegant expressions. (1995, 46).

Harvard's use of composition exams and its inclusion of writing instruction quickly became entrenched in the curriculum. While initially mandated for the sophomore year, the course eventually moved to the freshman year, and other courses in composition were offered across the upper years (although the vertical curriculum has not survived). From Harvard, the required composition exam and course spread quickly. By the start of the twentieth century, English composition was a common component of the curriculum at colleges and universities across the country. In many of these institutions, composition was linked with assessment because students took written entrance exams in composition, and remediation was required for those who did not perform adequately on the exams.

As the introductory composition course grew more prevalent in the university, it continued to exist within the frame around "acceptable practices" established by the Harvard offering. That is, it usually focused on themes isolated from broader rhetorical studies, and it continued to focus on error—in part because it was taught by lecturers, graduate students, or junior faculty, who had large numbers of students and tremendous workloads because of the many themes to grade. This combination of workload and evolving tradition led to another element of the frame, "the teacher as spotter and corrector of formal error" (Connors 1997, 142), which linked easily to another emerging frame during the rapid industrialization of the early twentieth century. This additional frame—which we referred to in the previous chapter as technocratic (and also has been called "administrative")—privileged management, efficiency, and tracking in education, as in industry and elsewhere. The work of psychologist E.L. Thorndike, for instance, suggested that education was in part a matter of developing conditioned responses to stimuli (1931, 162–166). As Mike Rose notes, Thorndike's enormously influential work in learning theory, combined with this emphasis on isolated practices, "suited educational psychology's model of language quite well: a mechanistic paradigm that studied language by reducing it to discrete behaviors and that defined language growth as the accretion of these particulars. The stress, of course, was on quantification and measurement" (Rose 2006, 186). Historians David Tyack and Larry Cuban (1995) also find evidence of this approach in the ascension of the "policy elite" to administrative positions in education. Members of this group became the "chief architects . . . of reform and arbiters of educational 'progress,'" and believed that educational progress (intimately tied to the nation's progress) "came in equally orderly statistics of success" (17).

Within this broader technocratic frame, the composition course fit perfectly. It was considered foundational and transitional, a site where students "lacking" particular skills needed for success in education could be efficiently and cheaply educated by low-status, entry-level workers (Brereton 1995, 22). This positioning of composition encouraged an emphasis on error because it allowed for an attention to the surface features, ignoring or undervaluing other aspects of writing—such as communication, content, organization, and style—which can seem more complex not only in responding but also in teaching and learning. Good writing, as a result, became defined narrowly as error-free writing (e.g., Connors 1997; Crowley 1998; Rose 1985). Students who successfully passed through the composition gateway could then be trained to become captains of industry. The number of sections and the number of students served also created a strong administrative component to the composition curriculum.

As this conception of composition became more firmly entrenched in the curriculum through the early decades of the twentieth century, writing instructors also became increasingly interested in framing—and refining—assessment practices so they would be more "efficient" and "objective." The focus was often on a text's individual features—mostly related to grammar, mechanics, and usage. There was a desire to standardize the reading and evaluation of writing, to devalue teachers' judgments, and to measure—to quantify—students' performance. In addition, there were concerns about efficiency because of the numbers of students being evaluated, whether in the classroom or beyond it. Thus, an emphasis on creating "scientifically respectable" means for evaluating essay exams developed, which led to the creation of intricate measurement scales (Witte, Traschel, and Walters 1987, 21). According to Rollo Lyman, at least seventeen scales were developed between 1910 and 1926, all attending to mechanical features such as spelling, punctuation, and capitalization, as well as content (Gere 1980, 115). While these scales reflect the emphasis, stemming from behavioralist learning theory developed by Thorndike and others, on translating scientific standards of objectivity to the evaluation of writing, Lyman explains that the frequent calls for more precise measures from these scales' developers illustrate the difficulty they faced "because there was no way of comparing a given piece of writing with one on a composition scale without calling the evaluator's opinion into play" (115).

To try to resolve this ongoing issue, Thorndike was actually involved in developing a popular scale for evaluating writing with his colleague Milo Hillegas. In 1912, Ernst Noyes wrote in support of the Hillegas scale in *English Journal*, explaining the framework supporting this approach to writing assessment:

> Now just as the study of business has produced the new application of science to industry known as scientific management, so the demand of the age for the measurement of results is bringing forth a new science of education based upon exact measurement and

judgment by ascertained facts. . . . If education has lagged behind business in testing theories by results, it has been because there has existed no adequate means of gauging skill in . . . [or] of estimating ability to write English. . . . Our present methods of measuring compositions are controlled too much by personal opinion, which varies with the individual. What is wanted is a clear-cut, concrete standard of measurement which will mean the same thing to all people in all places and is not dependent upon the opinion of any individual. (532–34)

Noyes continues applauding the scale developed by Hillegas and Thorndike because it "makes a uniform scale of measurement *applicable universally*" (emphasis in original) and marks "a great advance toward precision in rating composition" (1912, 534-35). Other researchers were also working within this frame to bring scientific objectivity to writing assessment. Starch and Eliot (1912), who conducted one of the earliest published studies on reliability and written composition, concluded that teachers could not agree on the grades for the same papers.

Along with the quest to develop more objective means of evaluating essays, the early twentieth century also saw the movement toward common entrance exams for colleges and universities. (Originally, each institution created and evaluated its own entrance exams.) The College Entrance Examination Board (CEEB)—later known as the College Board—was formed in 1901 and grew in membership and influence throughout the century. (Originally, membership of the CEEB consisted of the elite eastern colleges, but it became more inclusive over time.) The formation of the CEEB and the move to common entrance exams also illustrated the values of efficiency, standardization, and objectivity that were associated with the administrative approach to education and that marked the emerging field of psychometrics and the philosophy of positivism. Hand in hand with the emphasis on "data," the CEEB's formation also highlighted the devaluing of teacher judgments, since it emphasized a standardized test over the secondary teachers' judgments of academic performance (O'Neill, Moore, and Huot 2009, 17).

The CEEB's testing arm, the Educational Testing Service (ETS), was founded in 1947, with the first versions of the SAT given in the 1940s. The popularity of the SAT "signified a partial surrender of the right" of English professionals "to define academic literacy to psychometricians whose professional loyalties were in no way guaranteed to coincide with English studies specialist" (Traschel 1992, 118). In terms of framing, then, the CEEB and its standardized entrance exams contributed to the technocratic framing of education and achievement and the emphasis within education on psychometric measures, a frame that still influences educational policies and practices today.

As the CEEB and its work on common entrance exams grew, so did the culture's enchantment with psychometric technologies, such as multiple-choice test formats and statistical formulae. The so-called indirect methods of assessment codified in the exams led to multiple-choice tests of grammar, mechanics, usage, and other editing-related issues replacing (or complementing) tests that required students to compose essays. Then, as now, raters were trained to agree on a scoring guide (or rubric) and then monitored throughout the scoring session. The scoring protocol, in essence, attempted (and continues to attempt) to control the individual reading processes of the individual graders, standardizing it in much the same way that the test administration is standardized. In some cases, essay exams and multiple-choice exams were both used with statistical formulas employed to produce composite scores.

By the mid- to late twentieth century, while writing teachers favored essay exams, multiple-choice testing was entrenched as the dominant approach for making judgments about students' writing abilities. For example, ETS researchers in the early 1960s (e.g., Palmer 1960; Diederich, French, and Carleton 1961) made the same claim about evaluation of student essays as Starch and Eliot had in 1912: evaluators couldn't agree on the rating of student texts. Five years later, another group of ETS researchers published a study that detailed how they were able to get acceptable levels of agreement (reliability) among graders through holistic scoring (Godshalk, Swineford, and Coffman 1966). The privileging of decontextualized writing and evaluation, of course, is still popular today as evidenced by standardized exams such as the writing portion of the National Assessment of Educational Progress (NAEP), the writing section of the SAT, the popularity of tests such as ACCUPLACER and COMPASS for placement into college composition, and the emergence of ACT's Collegiate Assessment of Academic Proficiency and Progress (CAAP) and SAT's Measure of Academic Proficiency and Progress (MAPP), both intended to be used as tests to measure the progress of postsecondary students.

But this approach to (writing) evaluation, emphasized in the technocratic frame, contrasts sharply with the way rhetoric and linguistic theories frame writing and writing assessment. While timed, impromptu essays exams and multiple-choice tests about editing and language conventions continued to be used throughout the twentieth century (and into the twenty-first century), by the 1990s, writing portfolios had gained in popularity within writing classrooms for both teaching and assessment. The reasons for the popularity of portfolios for assessment are many, including their ability to support teaching. Peter Elbow and Pat Belanoff, in several publications (Elbow and Belanoff 1986a and 1986b; Belanoff and Elbow 1986), seemed to lead the way for compositionists to embrace portfolios as an assessment method. Elbow and Belanoff replaced a traditional composition exit test, which was a timed, impromptu essay exam, with a writing portfolio compiled from the work done as part of the coursework. They argued in *College Composition and Communication* that proficiency exams such as the one at their institution send "the wrong message about the writing process" (Elbow and Belanoff 1986a, 336). They claimed that the essay exam "can't give a valid picture of a student's proficiency in writing: we need at least two or three samples of her writing—in two or three genres at two or three sittings" (336). To replace the essay exam, they developed a portfolio system of evaluation in which students submitted portfolios and instructors worked in small groups to evaluate the portfolios. By the early 1990s, there was growing sense of enthusiasm for writing portfolios as a theoretically consistent method of assessing writing. Roberta Camp (1993) explained that the traditional essay exam format conflicted with the theoretical framework of writing that had been constructed by recently published research such as that by Flower and Hayes (1980, 1981), Applebee (1986), Bruffee (1986), Durst (1999), Berieter and Scardamalia (1987), and others. Portfolios, on the other hand, could accommodate this understanding of writing. Camp (1993) described some of the limitations or challenges with portfolios from a traditional psychometric approach when they were used for large-scale assessment but acknowledged that evolving psychometric theories of validity could work with portfolio assessment to change the model of direct writing assessment.

The next decade saw a variety of uses and investigations of assessment portfolios so that by the turn of the century, most compositionists (as well as other literacy scholars) saw portfolio assessment as the preferred method for collecting student writing samples. Reliability, however, continued to be a sticking point. By 2005, Edward White, an influential voice in composition circles who expressed reservations about the use of writing portfolios for large-scale assessment, admitted that portfolios "fostered revision, and offered much increased validity by using multiple writing samples over an extended period of time . . . teachers committed to teaching writing as a process rejoiced to find an assessment tool that welcomed drafts as well as final copies" (582). However, White also pointed out that portfolios presented some challenges, especially in terms of reliability and the cost of scoring, which hampered their use in large-scale situations. (We provide more detail about portfolios as an assessment method below.)

This very brief (and necessarily partial) overview of how composition (and writing assessment) was introduced into the college curriculum and of some of the implications of that introduction highlights how writing, writers, and writing assessment have been traditionally framed. Writing is typically seen as a skill that enables transcription, instead a process and series of strategies that enable thinking and meaning making. Good writing is marked by conformity to conventions and correctness. Good writers are those who can compose quickly on a topic off the tops of their heads, producing relatively clean texts through a single-draft process. Writing assessment, then, can (and should be) be standardized, objective, and efficient; and the results of writing assessment should be generalizable. These frames have remained powerful, still influencing how many constituencies perceive writing and assessment.

One of the implications of this approach to writing in general, and writing assessment in particular, is the valuing of efficiency, objectivity, and standardization driven by "expert professionals"—and the devaluing of the judgment of the individual classroom teacher—which has echoed across the decades as more and more standardized educational testing has not only been required but has also gained more significance in determining success and failure. Ironically, this inverse relationship between "professional expertise" and teacher authority reflects, and was in part driven by, a move during the early twentieth century to create a separate class of academic professionals inside colleges and universities and to establish their work *as* professional. That is, there was an effort to define the work of members of the academy, especially their methods and knowledge bases, as something that could be understood only with particular professional training and that could be itself judged—assessed—only by peers who shared this specialized knowledge. Assessment, of course, also became a distinct discipline with psychometricians, or educational measurement experts, as the authorities on acceptable theories and practices. Paradoxically, then, while the professionalization of academe had the effect of solidifying the boundaries around specialized academic disciplines within the academy, it simultaneously undermined the authority of individual teachers and contributed a technocratic, administrative view of teaching and learning (Bender 1993; Carey 1978).

The devaluing of teacher knowledge and the assertion of administrative, technocratic authority encompass all of education as evidenced but rather encompass all of education as evidenced in reports such as *A Nation at Risk* (U.S. Depart. of Ed. 1983) and *A Test of Leadership* (Miller et al. 2006), as we discussed in chapters one and two. However, composition has a history of being on the front lines of educational reform (as in the 1870s at Harvard). This was also true during the late 1940s and 1950s with the influx of students encouraged by the GI Bill, and the open admissions policies of the late 1960s and 1970s (e.g., Soliday 2002).

Composition is especially vulnerable in these policy discussions because it continues to be framed as it was in its formative years—as a universal requirement and a basic or foundational first-year course intended to prepare students for something beyond composition itself. Mike Rose, who has long focused on (and worked against) manifestations of writing and "remediation," observes that "bold, new proposal[s]" to remove or distance writing education (and other foundational courses) from college appear regularly, noting that "[a]cademicians for centuries have been complaining about the poor preparation of their students, the burden of introductory level teaching, and the overall decline of higher education" (2009, 118–119). "These professors," says Rose, "engage in a certain kind of . . . crisis talk that distorts the historical and social reality of American higher education, narrowing rather than encouraging careful analysis of higher learning in a pluralistic democracy" (119). In these discussions, composition is presented as a class taught predominantly by contingent instructors (part-time, non tenure-track and graduate students) who, if they are lucky, will be rewarded by moving out of the composition classroom and into literature, advanced writing, and/or graduate teaching. Many placement and assessment tests contribute to this frame, often serving as institutional gatekeepers by focusing on "proficiency assessment." Compositionists and writing assessment specialists, however, have struggled to frame composition and assessment in very different ways than have been promoted by traditional psychometric theory and an administrative approach to education.

CONTEMPORARY FRAMING OF COMPOSITION AND WRITING ASSESSMENT

While the technocratic frame and its attendant administrative approach to learning dominated educational theory and the development of assessment instruments, even in the early twentieth century there were alternative approaches to learning. One example of an alternative comes from Fred Newton Scott, who served as head of the Department of Rhetoric at the University of Michigan in the late nineteenth and early twentieth centuries. Scott published widely in composition, communication and journalism, and music (he wrote songs for the University and its various athletic teams). Some of his works, such as textbooks co-authored with Ohio State University colleague Joseph Denney, seem in some ways to reflect a typically current-traditional approach to writing instruction. However, Scott's essays—collected in books like *The Standard of American Speech*—as well as his course syllabi attest to the ways in which he approached composition and rhetoric instruction from a different perspective. Donald Stewart and Patricia Stewart outline Scott's approach (quoting Scott in part):

> [Scott] had an organic view of education, and it led him in the field of composition to the fundamental function of rhetoric. Where others were busy merely correcting grammar and spelling, he concluded that "the main purpose of training in composition is free speech, direct and sincere communion with our fellows, that swift and untrammeled exchange of opinion, feeling, and experience, which is the working instrument of the social instinct and the motive power of civilization." This definition was revolutionary at a time when it was unclear to others that rhetoric and its partner, composition, were even legitimate intellectual fields. (1997, 2).

Scott, along with peers such as Gertrude Buck (who was also his student), Joseph Denney, and Edward Hopkins, drew on a

wide range of emerging research fields in teaching and scholarship, including anthropology, biology, linguistics, physiology,
and anatomy (Mastrangelo 2010). Scott used this new research
to support his desire "to make rhetoric a legitimate field, insist-
ing it was a science, not an art," and he took an empirical
approach to language issues that was "certainly unique in his
time" (Stewart and Stewart 1997, 3).

In the frame advanced by Scott, language was social, contextual, and grounded in community. Language had the power to
change individuals and to effect change in broader contexts,
as well. Thus, Scott argued that when well taught, composition "arouse[d] in the pupil feelings of health, power, sanity
and hope—the invariable attendants of mental growth." (qtd.
in Stewart and Stewart 1997, 2). He reasoned that teachers of
composition were inspired, in part, by "the knowledge that from
[their] teaching men and women have gained power—power
to strike hard blows for truth, good government and right living" (qtd. in Stewart and Stewart 1997, 3). A gifted teacher,
Scott was known for leading students to "discover" their subject, and he believed that "even an untrained student lacking any special gift could write meaningful prose if properly
encouraged and stimulated" (Stewart and Stewart 1997, 4).
When working from this approach, Scott's pedagogical materials emphasized that language development would occur only
through the identification and development of subjects meaningful for the student, and that education should foster connections between those ideas and the educational context (Scott
1926). An active scholar, Scott was also involved in professional
organizations where he attempted to advance this frame—he
served as president of the Modern Language Association, the
National Council of Teachers of English (in fact, he was not only
NCTE's first president but also its only two-time president), the
American Association of Teachers of Journalism, and the North
Central Association of Secondary Schools.

In relation to his work with this last organization, as well
as others, Scott opposed the standardized entrance exams

for college admission being promoted by the Committee on Uniform Entrance Requirements. He argued instead for a close relationship between secondary schools and colleges, an "organic" model that involved "a living body" with both the schools and colleges "inseparable members" (qtd. in Stewart and Stewart 1997, 75). According to Scott, this type of relationship was opposed to the "feudal system" that marked the entrance exam model used by Harvard and Yale. Scott found this approach, in which the colleges told the secondary schools to "fit pupils to pass" the examinations or the students were not allowed to enter, to be problematic because "it promotes teaching to the test regardless of the real educational needs of students" and "it deprives teachers of necessary independence and initiative" (Stewart and Stewart 1997, 75).

But despite Scott's active professional life, his ideas were not reflected in the dominant frames surrounding ideas of "appropriate literacy" and teaching practices as the fields in which he was engaged—English Education, writing instruction (as distinct from classical rhetoric), and journalism education—developed through the early twentieth century. Albert Kitzhaber reasons that Scott's "ideas were too new, his recommendations for change too fundamental to be generally accepted," and too many people found his ideas "strikingly unconventional" (1990, 69–70). Scott's framework, then, not only did not connect with the dominant one that focused on basic skills and exercises over communication, but conflicted with it. By early 1930, just twenty-seven years after he founded it and shortly after Scott's retirement, the University of Michigan's Rhetoric Department (which by this time was known as Rhetoric and Journalism) was dismantled: rhetoric merged with the English Department to form the Department of English Language and Literature, and journalism was housed in a new (and separate) Department of Journalism. Scott's approach to composition, framed by rhetoric, aesthetics, psychology, and linguistics, remained marginal to the current-traditional approach that dominated mainstream composition teaching and textbooks in the early to mid-twentieth century.

However, with the influx of alternative perspectives on language development that accompanied what Kitzhaber called the "rhetoric revival of the 1960s," scholars in rhetoric, linguistics, and the burgeoning field of composition rediscovered Scott's work and found connections between it and other influential research, such as that by Russian psychologist Lev Vygotsky (Kitzhaber 1990, 4), as well as ideas from classical rhetoric to twentieth-century studies of language and literacy. These theoretical frames are, in most cases, in contrast to those purporting a current-traditional approach to teaching and learning as well as to ideas held by the traditional psychometric community that dominates educational assessment—at least as represented by many of its practitioners and in many public policy debates (later we emphasize convergences among our theories and those in educational measurement). In general, contemporary writing professionals understand and frame writing as a process (a focus on the act of composing) as well as a product (a focus on the text produced). From this perspective, writing is both a social and cognitive communicative act. In developing this framework, composition draws primarily on rhetorical theory and linguistic research.

Rhetorical Theory

Because it is a rhetorical act, writing professionals situate writing within a rhetorical frame. This frame acknowledges that writing is a form of communication governed by the writer's purpose, the message to be delivered, the audience to be addressed, and the context surrounding the writer, audience, and text. The rhetorical frame deconstructs the notion that a text exists outside of its specific context. Textual meaning is bound by the context including the writer's purpose and the audience. While classical rhetoric does teach commonplace strategies or techniques, their use—and their effectiveness—need to be determined in light of the particular situation their use—and their effectiveness—need to be determined in light of the particular situation. A text may be transported to other situations, but its effectiveness and, in fact, its meaning, can only be determined in context (e.g., Bazerman 2004).

In the late twentieth and early twenty-first centuries, this rhetorical frame has been operationalized in rhetorically-based pedagogies. These approaches require explicit attention to writing for different audiences and purposes and within different contexts. In them, writers learn to analyze the rhetorical situation and to make appropriate decisions about all aspects of a text including style, organization, evidence, even grammar and mechanics, in light of the situation. This frame, in contradiction to one that emphasizes conditioned response, presumes that students cannot be taught an exact plan for every situation. Instead, they can develop the critical thinking skills to analyze each particular situation and to make appropriate choices based on the analysis. In keeping with the idea of rhetoric as a way to understand texts in context, the notion of text considers all types of genres including (but not limited to) literary (e.g., novels, essays), academic (e.g., scholarly articles, student writing), workplace (e.g., reports, memos), and personal (e.g., journals, letters). More recently, the idea of "the text" and "writing" encompasses nonprint digital forms such as web pages, presentation slides, blogs, and other types of digital texts that have appeared in the last thirty years. While composition and rhetoric scholars focus on all types of genres, as a field we tend to be most interested in nonliterary genres such as technical and scientific writing, workplace writing, legal documents, and student essays.

Contemporary applications of classical rhetoric also inform composition's emphasis on the process of composing—prewriting, writing, and rewriting—because rhetoric was first and foremost a method for composing, not analyzing. As Bizzell and Herzberg explain, traditionally rhetoric was primarily "intended to teach a practical art and to provide guidelines for discourse in several well-defined social, political, and artistic arenas (1990, 2). Of the five canons of classical rhetoric, composition emphasizes three—invention, arrangement, and style. Although current practice shares some basic assumptions and approaches with classical rhetoric, the classic approach to rhetorical education was more prescriptive and rigid while today's methods are more recursive and flexible.

Another way classical rhetoric has influenced contemporary composition is in the focus on real-world texts—such as creating legal texts or business or technical writing—as well as on the role that texts play in peoples' everyday existences in the worlds where they live. In ancient Greece and Rome, rhetoric was clearly associated with civic engagement and public discourse. The goal of studying rhetoric was to use it to engage in public discussions and debate. Participation in the public discussion (whether legal, governmental, or ceremonial) for a variety of purposes (whether defending oneself or determining public policy or celebrating a war hero) was valued and expected (of course, not for everyone, but for the ruling classes). Contemporary composition has also embraced the idea of public discourse, encouraging students to tackle real-world topics for real audiences and purposes as a way of being involved in the world. This emphasis is apparent in first-year composition and advanced writing courses as well as in research and program administration.[3] The field's long-time commitment to basic writing also demonstrates the belief that being able to write is critical to success in the academy and beyond (e.g., National Commission on Writing 2003, 2004, 2005).

Linguistics and Literacy

Although composition as a contemporary field is grounded in classical rhetoric, it has also been significantly influenced by research in sociolinguistics and literacy. According to contemporary linguistic theory, everyone has the capacity to formulate language in order to communicate with others unless the individual has a disability. People build on this capacity by learning

---

3. A search of "service learning" using CompPile (http://comppile.org/search/comppile_main_search.php), a database of composition-related scholarship, identified 320 sources related to service learning across different types of writing courses and programs searched January 10, 2010).

how to communicate effectively—that is, how to formulate language using the conventions of communities where communication circulates within distinct contexts. From this perspective, the assumption is that students arrive in our classrooms with a variety of linguistic competencies and experiences on which teachers can build. Learning language happens most effectively through authentic use—that is, through genuine communication. All language—including nonstandard dialects—is rule governed, and users learn these rules through use. Part of this learning process involves error: "[Linguists] have learned, in language teaching, that there is no way to learn a language without being wrong in it and without being *allowed* to be wrong in it as one learns the right forms" (Shuy 1981, 105, italics in original). This means that error is a natural part of learning and that as users learn the standard forms and structures of a language, they will make mistakes. Errors are part of learning, however, and are best addressed in context, as part of the writing process instead of through isolated drills and exercises which are framed by behaviorist theories (Rose 1985).

Because language is such a critical component of culture, language use, according to sociolinguistists such as James Gee (1996), is socially situated with meaning determined by the social context. In other words, to communicate effectively requires more than an understanding of the linguistic code (i.e., the vocabulary, grammar, mechanics, etc.); users also need cultural and social knowledge to make meaning. As language users, we know this from our own experiences. For example, consider this question from a father to his daughter: "Have you washed the car?" The question could mean different things depending on how he says it (tone, emphasis, etc.) and the larger context. The question could be a genuine request for information—did she or did she not wash the car? Or, it might be functioning as a reminder to wash the car. Or, it could be that someone washed the car and the father is trying to determine who did it. In short, we constantly navigate these kinds of linguistic situations without explicitly thinking about it. Miscues or misunderstandings, in fact, highlight just how dependent we are on extralinguistic factors for effective communication.[4]

Writing, however, must communicate without the vocal cues that help determine meaning with spoken language. In addition, written texts are often less tied (or are often perceived to be less tied) to the immediate context. In writing, we consider many textual aspects part of effective communication. For example, style, including voice, tone, and word choice, as well as graphic features—such as punctuation and paragraphs—all contribute to how a writer conveys meaning to the audience. Sociocultural context is still a necessary component of meaning making when reading and composing written language although written texts are often considered acontextual, especially in school settings (e.g., the generic research paper assignment). However, knowledge of the sociocultural context is often critical to understanding a written text. Jonathon Swift's *A Modest Proposal* is a famous example of how important extratextual information is to accurately understand the text's meaning. Not only are individual texts embedded in the social context, but genres are socially situated. They are "rhetorical ecosystems" that constrain how writers function, creating "social and rhetorical conditions which make possible certain commitments, relations, and actions" (Bawarshi 2003, 8–9). Not only is understanding the context necessary to accurately interpret texts, but it is also necessary for creating them. A rhetorical stance, which looks at particular texts in context, provides a framework for writing and reading that acknowledges the value of sociolinguistic factors in producing and interpreting texts. In teaching students to write—as well as to analyze texts—compositionists value not only the text itself but also the social context that surrounds it; therefore, we favor a rhetorical approach in both writing and reading.

While contemporary linguistic and genre theories help composition and writing instructors see how texts are socially

---

4. See Hanks (1995, especially chapters one and two) for an extremely lucid discussion of the implications of contexts and an exploration of theories of language and interpretation.

embedded, they also help us understand that the relationship between language and context is dynamic and complex. Language does not just depend on sociocultural contexts for meaning; it also shapes contexts and interactions. Again, this is apparent in our daily experiences with spoken language—and now with electronic formats such as email and social networks—but it is also true for more structured interactions. In school, for example, researchers have documented the way discourse patterns function in classroom settings. According to researchers (e.g., Cazden 2001; Gee 1996; Heath 1983; Mehan 1979), teachers and students often interact in predictable ways that influence students' learning as well as whether or not the students are successful academically. Jenny Cook-Gumperz calls literacy a social process for "demonstrating knowledgeability," not just the acquisition of cognitive skills (2006, 3). Findings from studies (e.g., Agnew and McLaughlin 1999; Heath 1983; Hull et al.1991; Hull and Rose 1990) demonstrate that students who do not know how to participate in the discourse patterns of the classroom can be labeled as deficient or difficult. The interaction between teacher-student language use and student learning can be especially important in writing because teacher feedback is tied to students' revision choices as well as to their overall understanding of writing and themselves as writers (e.g., Ball and Ellis 2008; Berkenkotter, Huckin, and Ackerman 1991; O'Neill and Fife 1999; Sperling and Freedman 1987).

Not only are classroom discourse patterns and expectations important to consider, but so are other sociocultural factors—such as gender, ethnicity, and class—that influence students' learning and writing. Researchers have documented the effects of sociocultural factors on students' educational literacy experiences (e.g., Ball 1997; Ball and Lardner 1997; Haswell and Haswell 1996). Both teaching and learning are affected by extra-textual components of language use although neither teachers nor students may recognize it, as the work of researchers such as Claude Steele and his collaborators (e.g., Cohen, Steele and Ross 1999; Perry, Steele and Hilliard 2003) have demonstrated.

Writing as a Process

Another significant aspect of contemporary composition theory is associated with writing as process. That is, writing as an activity, something one does, not as a static artifact. As we mentioned above, classical rhetoric influenced compositionists' interest in process—that is, in how writers produce a text; however, cognitive psychology and psycholinguistics also contributed to the process framework. Work by researchers (e.g., Flower and Hayes 1981; Perl 1979; Rose 1988; Sommers 1980) examines how writers produce texts. What do writers actually do when confronted with a writing task? What factors influence a writer's process—experience, genre, context, feedback, technology? What interventions (e.g., prewriting, sentence combining, peer review, minimal marking) improve the writer's performance in the final text? Research studies indicate that many factors matter to a writer and can, in turn, affect the writer's performance—that is, the product. A process approach frames writing as learnable and teachable. From this perspective, there is no longer a sense that "writers are born, not made." By unpacking the writing process, by learning what experienced successful writers do, composition teachers can teach students strategies and techniques to help them improve as writers and ultimately improve the texts they produce. While this aspect of composition theory may have, at times, fallen out of favor in terms of research, it has continued to be a significant aspect of pedagogy.

Although process research was critiqued by some because of its inattention to sociocultural theories supported by classical rhetoric as well as sociolinguistics, it is not, in fact, antithetical to these other theoretical frameworks. Although some practitioners attempted to isolate and regulate the writing into discrete linear steps, theoretically, such isolation is not warranted. In fact, contemporary genre studies research explores the differences in how writers negotiate the social and cultural spaces created by genres, which are, in effect, part of a writer's process (e.g., Bawarshi 2003; Bazerman and Paradis 1991). This is easily illustrated by thinking about the prewriting activities for a chemistry lab report versus a literary analysis paper. What the writers must do to prepare—to prewrite, in essence—for these disparate genres is readily apparent.

IMPLICATIONS OF THE RHETORICAL AND SOCIOLINGUISTIC FRAMES FOR WRITING ASSESSMENT

The framing of contemporary composition theory and pedagogy by rhetoric and sociolinguistics has implications for writing assessment. If, as these frames indicate, all texts are contextually determined, then context needs to be a significant component in the judging of a text—whether that text is student-generated for a classroom assignment or for a writing exam or produced by professionals, as in a scientific article, an advertisement, or a technical manual. Writing assessment has attempted to accommodate these rhetorical and sociolinguistic theories in various ways. For example, this framework has influenced contemporary essay exams through the development of prompts as well as the evaluation criteria. Rhetorically and linguistically influenced prompts specify a particular topic to be addressed for a particular audience and purpose, such as when students are asked to write a letter to the principal of the school about a specific topic (e. g. , school uniforms, lunch schedule, or field trips). In a college-level writing assessment, a prompt such as this may be adapted to writing a letter to a public official or a college administrator about a specified topic. A significant part of the evaluation of the writing is determined by whether or not the student writer addresses the specified scenario appropriately. Another common task for a writing assessment requires the writer to take a position on an issue, sometimes after reading a particular passage or text, as in Washington State's impromptu essay exam (Haswell 2001) or the written portion of the Collegiate Learning Assessment. This task would be evaluated in part based on the writer's understanding of the passage provided.

Theoretically, when using a rhetorical lens, the evaluation of writing is not based on generic qualities that apply across all situations but rather on specific criteria, with the context determining what is effective for a particular audience. Even features that seem generic—such as grammar, mechanics, and usage or use of detail and/or evidence—that are often found on rubrics and scoring guidelines should be defined by the specific situation, according to rhetorical theory. Sociolinguistic theory also supports this context-dependent evaluation because, as explained above, decisions about grammar, mechanics, usage, vocabulary, and other rhetorical moves depend on context and audience. Therefore, according to contemporary composition theory, there is no universal definition of "good writing." Rather, good writing needs to be defined by what is appropriate and effective for a particular audience, a particular purpose, and a particular context. What is appropriate—and effective—in terms of language choice, evidence, and organization for one audience may be very different than for another one. So, in theory at least, students asked to write a letter to a parent or peer or principal should make choices based on their knowledge of the specified audience. A letter written for a peer would be very different in tone, language, and mechanics than one written for a principal. In fact, students' perceptions of the principal—and the school context—would influence such a letter.

Of course, the real scenario for these prompts is the testing one, not the one given in the task, because the real readers are the test graders, not the one specified in the prompt. If the students do not realize this, then the prompt may backfire. Leo Ruth and Sandra Murphy (1984, 1988) researched this very phenomenon and detail how prompts have misfired when used with real students. They explain that

> the act of writing actually begins in an act of reading comprehension, and we usually assume that each reader is getting the same message to direct his writing performance. In fact, the very stability of our measure of writing ability rests on this underlying assumption of uniformity in the examinees' interpretation of writing topics. Unfortunately, this is a questionable assumption. (1984, 410)

Ruth and Murphy, based on their research, advocate for more nuanced error analysis in writing assessments that examine response error—that is, they urge studies that look more carefully at the ways responses vary from what is anticipated. This kind of analysis of topics includes looking at *instrument errors*, which "derive from linguistic features of the writing topic"; *respondent errors*, which "emerge through misreadings of the writing topic by the student writers and teacher/raters; and *contextual errors*, which are "procedural errors arising from students' failures to understand how rules of normal discourse may be suspended in a writing test" (1984, 411).

Glynda Hull and Mike Rose's "'This Wooden Shack Place': The Logic of an Unconventional Reading" (1990) demonstrates how "misfires" can happen at the college level when students are asked to interpret a text. The subject of the article, "Robert," had different cultural frames for interpreting the text—a poem by Garrett Hongo—than those expected in an American university English classroom. But in talking with Robert about his reading of the poem, Hull and Rose (1990) illuminate the complex relationships between attempts marked as "failures" and the real work of a writer or reader. While Hull and Rose's article is about a class assignment, the same kind of divergent interpretation that Robert produced can just as easily happen with an exam prompt. As Ruth and Murphy explain, in an essay exam, the topic functions "autonomously under carefully controlled 'standardized' conditions" so individual differences in interpretation cannot be addressed (1984, 410). If a prompt asks college students to write a letter to their parents asking them to add money to the students' school accounts, the student writers need to consider many different factors unique to their families and their relationships with their parents. If a task asks students to read a text and then analyze it or take a position in reference to the argument, their stances will be influenced not only by the text but by their own cultures and experiences as well as the culture of college. These examples, then, illustrate the complicated factors introduced into assessment through a frame that puts audience, purpose, and especially context front and center. The contextual nature of the students' writing as well as the evaluator's reading of the student texts are supported by composition's theoretical framework even if the testing context doesn't acknowledge it.

The contextually bound nature of all language communication is one of the reasons compositionists who work within this framework, which is dominant within the field, tend to support assessments that allow readers to understand (as much as is possible) entire composing processes, including explicit attention to the ways in which the writer's understandings of purpose, audience, and context have informed choices of content, form, evidence, and the uses of conventions of style, formatting, grammar, and mechanics. A portfolio approach to writing assessment typically includes the collection of various texts that have been selected from a larger body and are framed by an introduction, often a reflective cover letter. Together, these documents provide evaluators with a broader view of a student's writing performance and get a better sense of the context of the writer's understanding of the context in which the contents of the portfolio were produced. Depending on the directions, the writer can frame the portfolio to fit the assessment with extratextual details to help the evaluator understand the who, what, and why for the texts. This kind of metawriting also can provide insight into a student's understandings of rhetorical theory and how that understanding has influenced her or his choices and, ultimately, the final text. The writer's process may also be explicated in an introduction, and often portfolios include process work for some or all of the contents. Including preliminary work—or at least addressing it in the introduction or reflection—also gets at another important component of contemporary composition, writing as a process.

Process theory, which attends to the process that produced the text, values more than simply the final artifact. It looks at how a student got to the final, polished piece by considering questions such as these: What prewriting did the writer engage in? What kind of feedback did the writer receive and how did she use it? What changed between the drafts? Addressing these aspects of writing can provide insight into the student as a writer and directly connects to improving teaching and learning, which is one reason compositionists tend to argue against single, timed, impromptu essays. In the timed, impromptu essay exam, writers are required to use a condensed or abbreviated writing process, producing a single draft and limiting the conclusions that can be drawn about a writer's composing processes; if the exam requires that writers only respond to one prompt, the single sample makes drawing conclusions about a writer's performance over a variety of tasks and in a variety of contexts impossible.

While timed, impromptu, essays exams and multiple-choice exams about editing and language conventions continued to be used throughout the twentieth and into the twenty-first centuries, by the 1990s, approaches that enabled readers to understand the relationship between the writer's analyses of these contextual factors and the writing itself had gained in popularity within writing classrooms for both teaching and assessment, as we mentioned earlier. Interestingly, the research on portfolios attests to an important challenge writing instructors face when using portfolios at the local level versus their use in large-scale assessments. At the local (classroom or program) level, writing instructors have been able to frame portfolio assessment in ways that reflect the values of our field, privileging a view of literacy that sees practices as local, contextualized, and rooted in the identity of individuals and groups. Postsecondary writing instructors through the 1970s, 1980s, and 1990s adopted portfolios and celebrated their effectiveness and their power at this classroom and local level to subvert traditional psychometric values and methods and champion composition's.[5]

---

5. The literature on writing portfolios is extensive. A search of "portfolio" on CompPile (http://comppile.org/search/comppile_main_search.php), a database of composition-related scholarship, identified over 700 published works from 1971-2008 (searched on July 31, 2009).

But as portfolios are used for large-scale purposes, such as college placement (e.g., Daiker, Sommers and Stygall 1996; Decker, Cooper and Harrington 1993; Lowe and Huot 1997), proficiency testing (e.g., Elbow and Belanoff 1986; Roemer, Schultz, and Durst 1991; Thaiss and Zawacki 1997), and even state-mandated K–12 exams in Kentucky and Vermont, some researchers have noted that their use begins to reflect elements of psychometric theories, reflecting the technocratic frame. Murphy and Grant (1996), for instance, claim that portfolios in themselves "mean little" because it is "the individual decisions concerning what to put in the portfolio, who evaluates it and how, and what to do with the results, as well as the assumptions that underlie those decisions, that determine the value of an assessment for teaching and learning" (284). In other words, Murphy and Grant argue that in and of itself, portfolio assessment is not enough to reframe writing assessment: the traditional psychometric framework may remain in place depending on how the portfolio is defined and the other decisions made about how it is evaluated. Scoring portfolios using the holistic technology developed by ETS, Broad (1994; 2000) argues, perpetuates the traditional psychometric framework and is contradictory to the theories that inform the portfolio.

But despite these attempts to place the use and scoring of portfolios within larger discussions of frames surrounding assessment, portfolios used for large-scale assessments continue to be scored much like essay exams in the early and mid-twentieth century had been. Jeffrey Sommers (1993) and his colleagues contend that to obtain reliable scores, monitoring of the readers is even more critical with portfolio scoring than essay scoring and that speed and efficiency are a concern. Susan Callahan (1997) reports these same kinds of issues and concerns about reliability in required high school writing portfolios, noting that these problems compromise the potential pedagogical benefits of portfolios. While portfolios have been championed because they frame writing assessment that values writing as a complex, contextual, meaning-making activity, Broad (2003) found in a an empirical study of a college portfolio assessment that issues of grammar and mechanics superseded concerns about organization, content, and effect. In other words, even with composition's enthusiastic promotion of portfolios as a way to reframe writing assessment, the dominant frames constructed in the late nineteenth and early twentieth centuries have persisted, especially when portfolio assessment is expanded to units of analysis beyond the individual classroom or writing program.

Even within portfolio assessment processes that seem to exemplify the contextual framework preferred within the field of composition, there is sometimes tension between the use of portfolios at the classroom and program level and their use at the institutional level. This tension, too, harkens back to instances of contact between the contextual frame and the technocratic, efficiency-oriented frame (and the tension between teacher authority and authority located beyond the teacher, such as that asserted by "experts" or by the institution) that dominates discussions of education and assessment outside of composition. Callahan's (1997) extensive study of Kentucky's mandated portfolio used for accountability highlights the way the bureaucratic, administrative approach can undermine the theoretical and pedagogical rationale for using them. She concludes from her longitudinal study of an English department at one high school:

> During the first two years of the portfolio requirement, the Department of Education focused on the accountability aspect of the assessment, stressing the rewards and sanctions schools could expect based on their students' performance. The emphasis influenced the meaning that portfolios came to have for the faculty and students. . . . [The teachers] experienced the assessment as a test of their competence as a department and felt great pressure to produce good portfolios' scores but little incentive to explore ways portfolios might best be used in the classroom. Consequently, while the assessment portfolios did change the amount and kind of writing produced by Pine View students and the criteria to assess

student writing, it did not demonstrably alter the way student writing was understood or taught. (295)

Callahan points out that this approach to assessment led to an emphasis on the scores—what the administrators and education department staff valued—over the potential for teaching and assessing writing in the classroom (and department) that aligned with composition's theoretical and pedagogical frameworks.

In college writing programs, where portfolios are more locally controlled, this emphasis may be minimized; however, compositionists writing about these types of programs (e.g., Borrowman 1999; Sommers, et. al. 1993; White 1993, 2005; Willard-Traub et al. 1999) have typically identified issues such as reliability, cost, time (for reading), and other logistics (such as storage) as critical—and in some cases even determining—factors. That is, while rhetoric, linguistics, and process theories all frame composition, and therefore influence how compositionists approach writing assessment, other administrative issues—which are in fact related to these theories—also influence it. Although administrative concerns do need to be considered, the primary issue should be the effects on teaching and learning. In a study of program-wide proficiency portfolios in two different classes with two different instructors, Alexis Nelson (1999) illustrates how the rationale that supports a program-wide assessment portfolio may not function in the same ways in different classrooms—teachers always communicate their own understandings of the portfolio to students, and that in turn affects how students produce that portfolio. In other words, even if portfolios are "standardized" in terms of content and scoring, the effects of the portfolio on student learning are determined, in large part, by the way the teacher presents and integrates the portfolio into the classroom. In writing assessment this is particularly a concern because composition functions (and has functioned historically) as both a gatekeeper—a mechanism for sorting students who belong in the academy from those who don't—and a gateway—a mechanism for students underprepared or from historically marginalized groups to gain access to the university. There is tension between these two functions since sorting students is not a neutral activity, and compositionists tend to value the idea that all students should have access to higher education (and all that it implies) but that they should also be provided with the appropriate instruction to succeed. Therefore, writing assessment, as Karen Greenberg (1998) and others have noted, can be a means for identifying students' needs and providing information for addressing them. In this way, writing assessment, as Schendel (2000) has argued, can be considered a form of social action—much as Eliot framed it in the 1870s—because it is a means of changing, maintaining, or disrupting society and people. Large-scale testing may be aimed at providing access and insuring all students get the help they need (often the rationale for placement testing and even proficiency exams), but it may not function this way for all students depending on the way the assessment is framed and carried out.

Writing assessment, even portfolio assessment, needs to produce valid and reliable results, but determining exactly what this means is not simple. Traditionally, large-scale assessments tend to use outmoded definitions of validity and reliability, understood through a frame that privileges quantification and objectivity, instead of engaging in the theoretical discussions—and debates—that surround these concepts. Some composition scholars, such as Patricia Lynne (2004), have argued for rejecting psychometric concepts of validity and reliability while others (e.g., Broad 2003; Haswell 2001; Huot 2002; O'Neill 2003; O'Neill, Moore, and Huot 2009) have argued for drawing on a more complex, nuanced understanding as represented in the educational measurement community (e.g., AERA, APA and NCME 1999; Haertel 2006; Moss 1994). In the next section, we argue that not only can contemporary understandings of psychometric theory accommodate composition's frames but that they can also help us connect to the larger frames about education and assessment that operate in the public, which can help shift these larger frames so that they reinforce—or at least accommodate—composition's values, theories and pedagogies.

HOW CONTEMPORARY PSYCHOMETRIC THEORY
FRAMES WRITING ASSESSMENT

Because of the rhetorical and sociolinguistic principles that inform our teaching and research, compositionists value writing assessment for its potential to improve teaching and learning. However, this emphasis on improvement is situated within the concepts of context, purpose, and audience that serve as tenets of our field. These culturally situated factors stand in stark contrast to the conceptualizations of assessment at the core of technocratic/behavioralist/administratively generated research and practice. In this tradition, the purpose of assessment was (and still is in many situations) to determine the extent to which a conditioned response was being achieved, and to what extent changes in the delivery could influence the success rate of the conditioning. While researchers like Thorndike believed that the capacity of subjects plays a role in the success of the delivery, that success is determined by the mental capacity of the subject, not by any cultural factors that might contribute to learning (1931 24–27; 198–200). This framework, rooted in positivism, contends that there is an objective reality and that it is measurable, which contrasts with contemporary theories about the social construction of reality. Williamson (1993, 1994) argues that writing assessment practices continued to privilege the positivist approach even as our theoretical frameworks about language and writing shifted (as we described above). The earlier positivist frames were primarily focused on sorting and ranking of students, while most writing teachers and assessment practitioners are more interested in using writing assessment to improve teaching and learning.

Shepard (2000) argues that assessment is a critical component to learning within the social constructionist paradigm that frames contemporary education. Teachers of any subject, including writing, need to gauge how students are learning, not only for grading but more importantly to identify what to teach and how to teach it. Often, however, we as teachers perform this kind of assessment—which is more informal, intuitive, ongoing, and immediate—without being consciously aware of it. We embed it into our teaching—whether explicitly through assignments, quizzes, and tests or more implicitly through classroom discussions and reflection. This approach to assessment, which is intimately connected to our pedagogy, can seem at odds with large-scale assessment that is linked to accountability, high-stakes exams, and other formal types of testing, such as placement.

Portfolios have been seen as an attempt to bridge the gulf between large-scale testing and the classroom, but their potential can be undermined, as Murphy and Grant (1996) argue. Yet, by understanding assessment as primarily integral to learning and teaching, we can begin to reframe it and make stronger connections between what we do inside our classrooms and what happens beyond them. At the same time, to frame writing assessment so it supports and aligns with composition's values, composition needs to engage with the psychometric community, which is highly influential in large-scale testing and public policy debates. Writing assessment theories and practices need to be consistent with language and literacy research and theory as well as assessment theories. While these scholarly communities may seem at odds, recent scholarship (e.g., Broad 2003; Haertel 2006; Huot 2002; Kane 2006; Murphy 2007; O'Neill, Moore and Huot 2009; Parkes 2007) has articulated ways that key assessment concepts such as validity and reliability are consistent with the way composition frames writing and assessment.

The concern over the concepts and language of writing assessment has been an issue in composition studies for at least two decades (e.g., Camp 1993; Cherry and Meyer 1993; Huot 1990; Lynne 2004; White 1993; Williamson 1993). To begin reframing writing assessment, compositionists must begin to understand these critical terms, the values they represent, and how they apply to writing assessment if we want to be able to connect to the existing frames surrounding educational assessment and to join the public discussions about writing and writing assessment. Only by engaging in these discussions can we hope to shift the current frames—and their implications—surrounding writing pedagogy and assessment.

Validity, the critical component of a test or assessment, is key in developing frames that can accommodate the values and goals of both the measurement and composition communities. Measurement scholars consider validity to be an emerging concept that has been evolving over the last fifty years. It is not inherent in the test but rather refers to the results and their interpretation and use.[6] In other words, an assessment is not valid or invalid but rather it produces results that are more or less valid. To determine the validity of the results, assessors need to conduct validity inquiry, which requires examining both theoretical and empirical evidence. For example, in placement testing, our validity inquiry would be guided by a question such as "Does this assessment adequately place students into our writing program curriculum?" The question should be asked about the specific content of the assessment as well as its context—the institution, its student population, writing program, and curriculum. While different types of evidence are related to different aspects of the test—construct, content, and consequences, for example—validity itself is considered a unitary concept. All evidence is considered in reaching a conclusion about the validity of the test results although some evidence may be more influential than others, given the particular assessment's purpose and the context. According to Samuel Messick (1989), "Validity is an overall evaluative judgment, founded on empirical evidence and theoretical rationales, of the adequacy and appropriateness of inferences and actions based on test scores" (33).

---

6. See Kane (2006), Moss (1992), Shepard (2000), and the 1999 edition of the American Educational Research Association (AERA), American Psychological Association (APA), and National Council on Measurement in Education (NCME) for discussions about validity as a general assessment term for both historical and contemporary accounts. For earlier discussions, see Cronbach (1988, 1989), Messick (1989, 1989a) and Moss (1992, 1994). For validity as it specifically relates to writing assessment, see Huot (2002), O'Neill (2003), Broad (2003), Murphy (2007), and O'Neill, Moore and Huot (2009).

More recently, Michael Kane (2006) explains that validation addresses use and consequences as well as the plausibility of the inferences and assumptions. He writes: "Validation focuses on interpretations, or meanings, and on decisions, which reflect values and consequence. Neither meanings nor values are easily reduced to formulas, literally or figuratively" (18). This complex approach to validity and validation—which is aligned with rhetorical and sociolinguistic theories that frame best practices in composition—acknowledges the social and contextual nature of validity that must be considered in the design, use, scoring, and interpretation of assessment results.

In reference to validity and literacy assessment, Murphy (2007) argues that culture should be a factor in validity inquiry in addition to more traditional aspects such as content and construct. Cultural validity, she explains, acknowledges that sociocultural factors "shape student thinking and the ways in which students make sense of" assessments' content, form, and consequences; validity inquiry would explore how the assessment takes sociocultural factors into consideration (235). According to Salono-Flores and Nelson-Barber, "These sociocultural influences include the sets of values, beliefs, experiences, communication patterns, teaching and learning styles, and epistemologies inherent in the students' cultural backgrounds, and the socioeconomic conditions prevailing in the cultural groups" (qtd. in Murphy 2007, 235). Murphy reasons that "[h]ow students make sense of test items and test situations is at the heart of validity" (235). This aspect of validity is particularly relevant for writing assessment because all language use—even that associated with an assessment—is a sociocultural activity. Only through thoughtful, informed research that includes a variety of methods—as, for instance, Hull and Rose (1991), Agnew and McLaughlin (2001), Broad (2000), and Smith (1992, 1993) have conducted—can compositionists understand why students responded to a particular prompt or task in a particular way and what the consequences of the results are not just to students but also to programs, institutions, and other stakeholders. Perhaps students are bringing a different set of experiences and assumptions to the task, as Ruth and Murphy (1984, 1988) and Hull and Rose (1990) document; or, as Steele (1997) concludes in his research on stereotype threat, students' performances may be influenced by their experiences with the broader culture. Raters' judgments—like student performance—can also be affected by sociocultural and contextual factors as researchers have demonstrated (e.g., Ball 1997; Haswell and Haswell 1996; Smith 1993). To accurately interpret and use assessment results, it is critical to understand how the students' performance and the raters' judgments have been influenced by a multitude of factors.

Validity inquiry, then, is wide-ranging and ongoing, a conceptualization of this idea incorporated into the *Standards for Educational and Psychological Testing* published by the American Educational Research Association (AERA), the American Psychological Association (APA), and National Council on Measurement in Education (NCME), the leading organizations for educational measurement professionals: "As validation proceeds, and new evidence about the meaning of the test's scores becomes available," the *Standards* say, "revisions may be needed in the test, in the conceptual framework that shapes it, and even in the construct underlying the test" (1999, 9). The validation process starts with explicit statements about the conceptual framework, including the concepts or constructs being sampled; the knowledge, skills, abilities, processes, or characteristics being assessed; and how each construct is to be distinguished from other constructs and how it relates to other variables (9). The conceptual framework also takes into consideration the use of the test results and the consequences if a rationale for the assessment is that some benefit will come from the assessment's results. For instance, if an assessment claims it will result in an improvement of teaching —a common rationale for using program portfolios—then the validation inquiry needs to examine if teaching has improved (or not) as a result of the assessment, and there should be evidence to support the claim. In placement testing, a basic assumption is that students' needs are addressed more effectively in a developmental course; therefore, the validation inquiry must gather a variety of evidence to determine if, in fact, that is the case. When assessments are meant to enact some change—which is often a critical feature of assessment in the administrative and technocratic framework—then a "fundamental purpose of validation is to indicate whether these specific benefits are likely to be realized" (16–17). In the end, the validation process requires building an argument that addresses a variety of complex issues and draws on a variety of evidence and rationales.

While validity is the most critical component in determining the value of an assessment and its results, according to the measurement community, reliability is also an important concept. In writing assessment, reliability was emphasized in the behavioralist, objective approach that dominated most of the twentieth century. According to the *Standards*, reliability is "the degree to which test scores for a group of test takers are consistent over repeated applications of a measurement procedure and hence are inferred to be repeatable for an individual test taker" (AERA, APA, and NCME 1999, 180). In a review of reliability and writing assessment, Cherry and Meyer explain that reliability "refers to how consistently a test measures whatever it measures" (1993, 110). The consistency of a measurement can be influenced by the test design and administration, the students, and/or the scoring; however, in writing assessment, reliability often has been limited to discussions of the agreement among raters—interrater reliability (1993).[7] While reliability has been an important component of writing assessment, there has been little explicit discussion about how it contributes to validity, which is the more critical term. Haertel (2006), an educational measurement scholar, acknowledges reliability's concern with the quantification and precision of test scores and other measurements, but he also

---

7. Even in this narrow focus in reliability, there has been little consistency in how to determine interrater reliability and how it affects the results. For a more thorough critique see Cherry and Meyer (1993), Hayes and Hatch (1999), and O'Neill, Moore, and Huot (2009).

links it to validity: "Like test validity, test score reliability must be conceived relative to particular testing purposes and contexts. The definition, quantification, and reporting of reliability must each begin with considerations of intended test uses and interpretations" (65). He calls for "further integration of notions of reliability with evolving conceptions of test validity" (103). This explanation of reliability, which is much more nuanced than what Cherry and Meyer (1993) found in the published literature on writing assessment, frames reliability as a more restricted term than validity that must be considered in reference to the particular context and use of the assessment.

Writing assessment specialists have explored reliability in this way (e.g., Broad 2003; Haswell and Wyche-Smith 1994; Hester et. al. 2007; Smith 1992, 1993), but as a field, we can and should do so more thoroughly. Moss argues, specifically in reference to portfolios, that "less standardized forms of assessment . . . present serious problems for reliability, in terms of generalizability across readers and tasks as across other facets of measurement" (1994, 6). Though carefully trained readers can achieve acceptable rates of reliability, with "portfolios, where tasks may vary substantially from student to student, and where multiple tasks may be evaluated simultaneously, interreader reliability may drop below acceptable levels for consequential decisions about individuals or programs" (6). Moss concludes that "although growing attention to the consequences of assessment use in validity research provides theoretical support for the move toward less standardized assessment, continued reliance on reliability, defined as quantification of consistency among independent observations, requires a significant level of standardization" (6). However, less standardized forms of assessment are often preferable "because certain intellectual activities"—such as writing— cannot be documented through standardized assessments (6).

Moss (1994, 2007), in fact, does not simply reject reliability but rather suggests that literacy scholars and assessors look beyond psychometric theory to address the limitations associated with traditional conceptions of reliability. In other words, when less standardized forms of assessment are preferable, she suggests rethinking reliability and how it contributes to validity. This rethinking—or in our terms, reframing—can happen when we shift the frame away from the methods associated with determining reliability (which involve statistical formulae and standardization) and toward the values the term represents. These values, according to Jay Parkes, include "accuracy, dependability, stability, consistency, or precision" (2007, 2). In Parkes' argument, a "reliability coefficient is a piece of evidence that operationalizes" these values (2). This shift to a focus on values, according to Parkes, also shifts the focus of ideas associated with "reliability" from methods, which are most often associated with statistics and quantification, to concepts that "serve as evidence of broader social and scientific values that are critically important in assessment" (2). Depending on the context and use of the assessment, other methods—beyond demonstrating an acceptable interrater reliability coefficient—may be more appropriate to support a reliability argument. The key, Parkes contends, is to build an appropriate argument for the methods used that demonstrates that the assessment results are, for instance, accurate and dependable for the particular use. This argument, as with a validity argument, should include both theoretical and empirical evidence.

Parkes illustrates his argument by describing how his approach could work in a classroom where the teacher is evaluating students' development of collaboration skills based on a two-month science project. Parkes outlines the specific components of a reliability argument and explains how it would work using this example.[8] Smith (1992, 1993) takes a more nuanced approach to reliability by looking beyond interrater reliability, and as a result develops the expert reader system for evaluating placement essays. Others (such as Haswell and Wyche-Smith 1994; Lowe and Huot 1997; and Hester et al. 2007) take a similar approach and explore both the methods for evaluating student writing

---

8. For a more extended discussion of how Parkes' approach would work in writing assessment, see O'Neill (n.d.) and O'Neill, Moore, and Huot (2009).

(essays and portfolios) and the theoretical frameworks that inform the assessment and the use of the results. In these examples, determining reliability goes beyond a statistical formula and makes a substantive contribution to the validation process.

While these discussions of assessment theories and terms such as *validity* and *reliability* may seem separate from the day-to-day issues of teaching and learning that writing instructors and program directors face, they are actually closely related to those issues. For writing specialists to begin reframing, we need to have a sound understanding of the theories and values that have shaped—and continue to shape—the teaching and assessment of writing. However, this knowledge alone is not enough. If it were, neither K–12 nor higher education would be feeling the pressure from policymakers and the public for accountability through assessment. We also must learn how to communicate our knowledge effectively beyond our own discipline and specialties so we can affect the discussions being held in state legislatures, departments of education, corporate boards, policy commissions, and public forums. Because these discussions—which are happening beyond our educational institutions in a variety of settings from legislatures to think tanks to corporate board rooms to public forums such as newspapers, websites, and radio talk shows—can have serious consequences to both teaching and learning, we need to develop ways to engage in these broader conversations. The next chapter takes up strategies and techniques for effectively engaging in these broad-based discussions within the context of our local situation.

4

REFRAMING STRATEGIES
AND TECHNIQUES

In chapter two, we described the current frames surrounding discussions of higher education, and stories linked to them. Their central concepts, conveyed in words and phrases like "preparedness" and "college and career readiness" are linked to a number of broader, interrelated stories. Within an ever-expanding frame that constrains the range of meanings and actions that can be "commonsensically" associated with these concepts, some approaches to teaching, learning, and assessment are seen as "logical" and others as "illogical," "impractical," or "uncommonsensical." We like the way linguist William Hanks describes how people function when these frames become taken-for-granted. He says that in them, "native actors . . . are curiously comfortable amidst an infinity of assumption, beneath a horizon as familiar and unnoticed as a night sky" (1995, 5). Their perceptions of "what is," and the stories that they tell based on those perceptions, become "reality."

The current stories being told about education, we contend, present some vexing issues for postsecondary writing instructors, program directors, department chairs, and others who want to reframe writing assessment. First, they suggest that while the purpose of education is to prepare students for citizenship, neither instructors nor the educational system understand what is needed for twenty-first-century citizenship and thus cannot adequately fulfill that mission. Second, they say that, in school, students develop the means they need to reach an end that is defined for them—means often described in terms of "college and career readiness," or "skills," or "tools." Many contemporary policy reports focusing on education ask not *whether* achieving ends that have been defined for students (such as preparation for college and career) is an appropriate goal, but how students should reach those ends, through what means (see Adler-Kassner and Harrington, n.d.). These reports are dominated by what has been called a technocratic approach (e.g., Boyte 2005; Labaree 1997), which privileges efficiency. This leads to a story whereby teachers and the educational system are to be held accountable for the development of necessary skills, and proof that we have done our jobs will come from students' performances on exams—certainly national ones, and perhaps standardized as well (Miller 1991, 23). Third, the current stories being told about education infer that the structure upon which disciplinarity, academic credibility and, to some extent accreditation, is based is problematic. Finally, they lead to questions about the purposes of and audiences for assessment. One result of these different stories has been a bifurcation in discussions about assessment. For some, it is an internally focused process intended to help those inside the academy improve student learning. For others, it is (or should be) an externally focused process intended to generate data that proves to stakeholders outside the academy that particular kinds of learning are being achieved.

But literacy educators have long raised questions about the need for *un*common sense, the need to question traditional approaches to literacy education that tend to extend from narratives about career preparation and efficiency rooted in the late nineteenth and twentieth centuries. Alternatives to these approaches have been developed by people who have had "the capacity to question received wisdom—to ask why and not be satisfied with the conventional answer" (Mayher 1990, 3). In this chapter, we take Mayher's cue and present strategies that writing instructors, program directors, and others concerned with writing instruction and administration at the postsecondary level can use in a quest to work outside some of the common assumptions reflected in the questions asked in assessment, the methods used to respond to those questions, and the responses resulting from those questions and methods. These strategies are adapted from media strategists and community organizers who have themselves been long involved with this work of questioning commonsense assumptions and looking for alternatives to conventional answers.

STRATEGIES FOR ACTION: FRAME-CHANGING BASICS 101

As we argued in chapter two, for teachers who want to reframe writing assessment, an awareness of the "infinity of assumption" accompanying larger narratives about the purpose of education, and the function of efficiency within that narrative, is crucial. This narrative forms the "night sky" that spans above us as we undertake work in the academy and constitutes the outlines of a number of stories that shape our work—about what education is for, what students should do, and how teachers should teach them to do those things. If contemporary policy and media reports are to be believed, "everyone" agrees on the purpose of education—it's to prepare students for college and careers. A Google search using the term "college and career readiness" yields over 50,000 results; results on the first page alone come from Achieve (2008), a very powerful education think tank working to "reform" secondary education by creating narrowly defined curricular standards directed toward "college and career readiness" as determined by employers; the Texas, Illinois, and Massachusetts Departments of Education; the Oakland, California School District; and the National Center for Educational Achievement, a subsidiary of ACT that provides "school improvement products and services and data-driven best practices research" (and partners with, among other organizations, ACT and the Education Trust [both of whom are also partners of Achieve]).

Approaches to assessment also extend from this "infinity of assumption," of course, shaping and contributing to the familiar horizon of stories about students, education, and writing. Beyond the level of the institution, two versions of this narrative are evident. The dominant one, located in reports from groups like the Spellings Commission, focuses on "proving"—the need to define and determine the effectiveness of the means by which students are being prepared for "college and career." The American Diploma Project (ADP, a project in which Achieve is one of several partners), for instance, hired researchers to define "good jobs" using "factors such as entry-level salary; provision of benefits; and opportunities for further career advancement, education, and training" for a germinal report called *Ready or Not: Creating a High School Diploma That Counts* (Achieve 2004, 105). They further focused on careers determined to "represent 62 percent of the jobs in the next 10 years" (105). Then, they "made a deliberate effort to establish or refute potential connections between what students learn in high school and what knowledge and skills are necessary to be successful in the workplace" (106), checking their findings in consultation with partners from the National Association of Business, an early ADP partner, and the Educational Testing Service (106–107). (ADP also sought evidence from college faculty; however, faculty voices are less prominent in *Ready or Not* and almost unheard in subsequent materials published by Achieve.) Assessment here "logically" focuses on discerning how the ends outlined in these documents—ends largely defined by business partners—are being achieved by students, through classroom instruction, or within an institution. These approaches reflect a technocratic narrative that suffuses contemporary education and suggests that the purpose of education is to help students develop the means by which they can reach ends defined by twenty-first-century employers.

But while the approach outlined by ADP seems commonsensical, there are other approaches within policy circles to the larger idea that education is intended to help students develop the means to reach predefined ends. The most prominent of these, the initiative from the Association of American Colleges and Universities (AAC&U), called Liberal Education: America's Promise (LEAP), for instance, attempts to strikes a balance between the ideas that education should help students move toward such ends and should also contribute to their shaping based on local contexts and cultures (see http://www.aacu. org/leap/). LEAP's signature report, *College Learning for the New Global Century*, provides an alternative to the technocratic narrative located in reports like those from the Spellings Commission and ADP. "Today," it says, "powerful social forces, reinforced by public policies, pull students . . . toward a narrowly instrumental approach to college. This report urges educators to resist and reverse that downward course" (AAC&U 2007, 17) and makes the case that the ability to shape ends *is* one of the requirements for successful twenty-first-century citizens. "In a period of relentless change," the document notes, "all students need the kind of education that leads them to ask not just 'how do we get this done?' but also 'what is most worth doing?'" (13). The report continues, explaining that the knowledge-based economy will be fueled not by workers who can apply narrow skills to specific contexts, but by thinkers who can apply knowledge to broadly based concerns.

The idea that education is intended to help students develop means to ends, then, is a shared principle across these documents. However, there are points of disagreement within them. What elements constitute these means? (The ability to analyze audience expectations? Or the ability to produce a piece of writing with specific and predetermined boundaries, like a five-paragraph essay?) Who should develop what means? (Should everyone learn the same thing? Or, should different groups learn different things in different ways determined by their intellectual capacity? As indicated how?) And how should these means be enacted and applied? These differences extend to questions about assessment. Should assessment research ask how many students graduate in what amount of time? About what scores they achieve on (sometimes standardized) measures of learning? About how many students are retained? Alternatively, should they ask what students are learning in what courses, how they are learning, and how that learning could be improved? How or whether students are able to apply their learning in one course to their work in another?

While these aren't mutually exclusive groups of questions, they do emphasize different aspects of the educational process. The first batch focuses on *demonstration* of achievement—on proving that students are doing something that they are supposed to do. The second focuses on *discovering and improving* what students are doing in a process of schooling. The distinctions between these questions parallel differences we have seen in queries raised by administrators and writing instructors. On Linda's former campus, for instance, students chose whether they wanted to start in a first-semester, elective-credit writing course and then go on to the second-semester course, which was required for general education credit, through a process of guided self-placement (GSP). At one point, a visiting retention consultant insisted that the writing program needed to prove, through an examination of students' grades in later courses beyond writing, that GSP was "more successful" than using ACT scores for placement.

Linda and her writing colleagues argued that the number of uncontrolled variables in this metric were dizzying. They contended that there were several more relevant questions: Did GSP foster qualities that assessment and retention literature had shown to be crucial for student persistence, like self-efficacy? What qualities of critical writing, reading, and analysis were crucial as they moved through their courses at this institution and careers beyond? To what extent were these qualities cultivated in first-year writing courses and built upon in later courses? Data on these questions, Linda and her colleagues maintained, would speak both to instructors inside the writing program, who were invested in developing students' abilities in ways that would help them to be successful in the context of their university, *and* involve stakeholders outside the writing program in discussions about whether and how these qualities might be cultivated, and what changes could be made.

The differences in these assessment queries extend to different stories about learning. The retention consultant told a story about learning that involved quantifiable performance with parameters determined by someone outside the context of the institution. Linda and her writing colleagues, alternatively, told a story about learning that involved defining objectives for learning that were both situated and assessed locally. Further, in the local, situated perspective, the results of the assessment(s) would be used to improve the curriculum. These examples, then, embody the tension between the dominant story about writing education and assessment and possible alternatives to it. They raise important questions: What is the objective of an immediate decision like what writing course to take; of a longer-term process like a writing course or program; of a university-level education? What means are most effective to achieve those objectives? Who gets to outline those objectives? Who should get to determine how students work toward them? (People—or agencies—who write standardized tests? Students? The institution?) What qualities should be associated with evidence that this development is successful? Who should get to make decisions about these questions? (A retention consultant? Faculty in the discipline where questions about assessment are being raised?)

These are important questions. It's likely that, as writing instructors, we think that people who actually teach classes (like us) should shape the stories that affect what students learn in our classes and how they do that learning. At the same time, though, it's essential that we recognize that others outside of our classes and programs also have a heavy investment in what happens inside of them. From instructors in other departments, to university administrators, to future employers, to policymakers, people genuinely care about what students learn in writing classes. The challenge, of course, is to help those interested others understand that caring isn't necessarily enough; that when we say "writing is everybody's business," we don't mean that others get to tell us what to do, but that, since qualities of good writing are, in large part, context specific, we all share the responsibility of helping writers understand and work with the qualities of good writing in their specific contexts.

BUILDING ALLIANCES

"A Story of Us": A (Very) Brief History of Alliance Building in Community Organizing

While we might have stories we want to tell individually about writing instruction, teachers, or students, those stories won't go far unless they are connected to stories other people want to tell. That's because the stories that endure and form that "infinity of assumptions" reflect the values, beliefs, ideologies, and practices of a lot of people, not just one person or a small group. They become what community organizer and sociologist Marshall Ganz calls a "story of us" that allows people to move from the ways we think of ourselves as individuals and the stories important to us, to larger pictures and bigger stories that are important for others, as well (2001, 15). What we must do to reframe writing assessment is create a new "story of us" that brings together the interests and values of others and the values and interests we hold as individuals and as writing professionals whose work is rooted in research-based best practices. This new story can lead us *collectively* to a vision of the possible and to choices meant to enact that vision.

When it comes to assessment writ large, and writing assessment especially, it is extremely important that we be aware of the larger stories shaping contemporary approaches like those outlined above. Whether we like it or not, the technocratic narrative is extremely powerful in contemporary discussions of education. As during the period of rapid social, political, and technological change during the end of the nineteenth and beginning of the twentieth centuries, we are currently in the midst of shifts that challenge some of our most basic assumptions about space, time, and the circulation of ideas and information. The responses to these shifts also parallel those during the earlier period.

Within education, the movement to clearly define the purposes of a P–12 educational system that enrolls over fifty million students, graduates three million students yearly, and sees about two million of these students pursue postsecondary education (Stanford University Bridge Project n.d.) is seen as an urgent national priority. The idea that education should prepare students for "college and career readiness" is a convenient, accessible, and clear statement of this enormous system's purpose—whether or not the details of what that *means*, exactly, or how it will be carried out, are defined. To shape a story of us that brings together these interests and those of others, we must find ways to build connections between the positions we find important to those held by others, and from our stories to theirs, to collaboratively author a new tale.

Community organizers have long recognized the importance of making "a story of us"—of building alliances around shared stories—in their change-making work. Ganz (2001) finds examples of these efforts in literature from the Bible, to Aristotle's speeches, to *Henry V.* For our purposes, it is useful to see the legendary community organizer Saul Alinsky (1946), who began his organizing career in the Chicago area known as "Back of the [Stock]Yards" in the early twentieth century, as a starting place for creating these stories of us. Alinsky recognized that there could be no change, no power, without shared stories. He outlined a strategy for action that has been developed through the twentieth and twenty-first centuries by the Industrial Areas Foundation, the organization that grew out of Alinsky's original organizing work, and that has been adapted by countless other organizers and organizations.

This strategy starts with identifying individuals' passions and interests—what Alinsky calls self-interest, which he says "can be transformed from an obstacle into an advantage" as individuals realize that those interests are linked to a greater concern for others and for society (1946, 89-100). It then moves to linking individuals with *shared* self-interests, because there is always greater power in numbers and alliance. Since these individuals share collective passions and interests—and people are always motivated by those fundamental passions—they find greater community and motivation in their shared interests. Together, they then identify a target for action. What can they do—something achievable, something that will affect a positive change—that will advance that self-interest? An important part of this change making, though, is recognizing the importance of tactical compromise and pragmatic action. The most important element of this process, Alinsky says, was action. One of his (many) mantras is "All change means movement, movement means friction, and friction means heat." Fretting about long-term strategies—would this change be the right thing ten, twenty, fifty years from now?—interferes with the real issue, how to address problems right here and now. Similarly, the key for Alinksy is to construct alliances that serve the purposes of "the people" *now*. The alliances or purposes might shift down the road, but that isn't important.

In Alinsky's philosophy, the most important outcome of organizing is for people to recognize that when they identify shared concerns and work together to address these concerns, they can both effect that positive change, and recognize in themselves the power *to* effect change. Then, they should assess: how can they both celebrate their success and assess their strategies to be more effective next time? From this step, they can begin again, fueled by their success and ready to be more effective next time. The ultimate goals of Alinsky's approach to building a story of us are to bring people together to make change, and to help people recognize in themselves the *ability* to make change by working together.

ALLIANCE BUILDING/STORYTELLING IN ACTION

Since Alinsky's original organizing work at the turn of the last century in Chicago, his approach has spurred countless individuals and organizations to action. For all, the first step in this work is building alliances, and within that step it is possible to identify three approaches used by organizers that postsecondary writing instructors and program directors can adapt. Each of these approaches shares a common core that involves forging connections around individuals' and groups' interests, working on issues related to those interests, and taking values into consideration. The differences between the approaches lie in the extent to which they emphasize short-term action and achievement of immediate projects, or long-term values that lead to accomplishment of bigger picture goals (see Adler-Kassner 2008 for more on these approaches).

When it comes to reframing writing assessment, these are important considerations. It might be valuable to agree to an assessment project that is potentially problematic, for instance, if it will lead to more faculty lines for the writing program. On the other hand, it might seem more important to resist such an effort, despite potential costs, if it violates principles that are seen as important within the program and that affect student learning. These are the kinds of choices that present themselves within these different approaches; with their different emphases, each brings opportunities and challenges.

Interest-Based Alliance Building

Interest-based organizing is the approach most closely aligned with Alinsky's work, and it underscores efforts of the organization he founded, the Industrial Areas Foundation (IAF). The end goal of interest-based work is to help people recognize and cultivate their own interests in and talents for change making, because the assumption is that work is most effective, representative, and beneficial when everyone comes together around their shared common interests. The benefit of interest-based alliance building is that it helps people quickly establish their connections to one another; the potential challenge, though, is that the projects that extend from it might be very short-term and not lead to sustained alliances or actions.

Since the emphasis here is on building connections that are based in self-interest, the first step in alliance building in this approach is to learn about peoples' passions, because those passions hold the keys to involvement. Organizers learn about these stories by having one-to-one or small group discussions that help the organizer to learn about what fires people up. The initial questions organizers ask are few, but important: What do you care about, and why? What motivates you to action around these issues? Once organizers have identified issues people care about, they move to the next step, connecting people around their interests: community jobs programs, the installation of lights on a dark street, even changing the size of the rocks next to a railroad bed that people must cross to get to work (Adler-Kassner 2008, 101).

Linda came across an example of this in her own backyard. In 2009, homeowners in her neighborhood were required by the city to replace cracked sidewalk squares. One of her neighbors, a consummate lay organizer, distributed a 3x5 flyer to every house in the area that read, "Join Your Neighbors for Cheaper Sidewalk Repairs." This is a great illustration of interest-based organizing—people are passionate about saving money, especially in southeastern Michigan's battered and bruised economy, so this was a cause around which they were happy to rally. But the person doing the organizing also then got to talk with neighbors about other issues that were important to them, trying to get them to work together on those, as well. For interest-based organizers, the key is to help others realize that when they come together around their passions and interests, they can effect change. As they recognize they have this power, they become empowered to be more involved, effect more change. This change always stems from their interests and passions, though; their motivations aren't especially relevant. Change by change, working person to person, the world becomes a better place as people work to improve their situations.

Reframing activities that extend from an interest-based approach have as their goal bringing together as many people as possible—students, instructors, faculty, administrators, staff, community members—in a discussion about writing instruction and assessment, and helping people find common areas of interest (and action) around issues related to writing (and assessment). In this model, the program director, department chair, or writing instructor who seeks to facilitate alliance building is primarily a conduit—his interest is in fostering connections, but *not* in advancing any particular (short-term) agenda of his own, save for bringing people together and having the confidence that, working collectively, they will identify positive goals for change.

Values-Based Alliance Building

Where an interest-based approach revolves around alliances built on shared interests, a *values-based* one begins with cultivating shared values. That's because, in this approach, cultivating and acting upon those shared values is seen as key—from values extend actions, and from actions come change. As George Lakoff, whose work is often associated with this model, notes, "Issues are secondary—not irrelevant or unimportant, but secondary. A position on issues should follow from one's values, and the choice of issues and policies should symbolize those values" (2006, 8).

Because values-based alliance building begins with identifying the fundamental suppositions underscoring actions and beliefs, its practitioners tend to begin by listening and/or reading to understand the ideas others embrace and the ideologies underscoring them. This might mean asking people about what makes them passionate or fires them up, as in an interest-based approach, but from a values-based perspective, the person asking the questions would be listening and/or looking for deeper frames, deeper values, underscoring those passions. If Linda's neighbor were working from a values-based perspective, for instance, he wouldn't be distributing flyers about the immediate issue of sidewalk repairs; instead, he might write a manifesto about the importance of citizen action and distribute that, inviting others who share his commitment to the value of citizen action to come to a meeting. Together, they might outline principles related to that frame of citizen action; ultimately, through that frame, they would identify issues upon which to focus. The issues, though, would come after the outline of the frame was completed. Because it has grown up through communication studies, linguistics, and frame theory, values-based alliance building extends in many ways from semiotic theory and the study of language, resting on changing values associated with language and/or the language itself. Where interest-based organizing has its eye on short-term action, then, values-based work is focused first on long-term change. Success is achieved only when the *values* associated with an issue are addressed successfully.

For the instructor or program director who wants to use a values-based model for her work, identifying *her* values and those of the program is a crucial first step. What are the core principles, the things that are absolutely most important for and about writing and writers, and why are those core? Sometimes these values are expressed explicitly in institutional documents such as mission statements; other times they are implied by actions and agendas of individuals or programs. Once principles are identified, she can start identifying people (and organizational units) who potentially share those values and begin to build alliances with them. Through alliance building and discussion, she and her allies eventually identify issues they would like to address together. Her role is to make sure that her values remain primary; to do so requires her to endorse the importance of those values over other values and to persuade others that those values are more important.

The values-based model might, at first glance, seem most attractive to writing instructors and program directors who want to reframe writing assessment. We might want to start here, for instance, when we feel like the things *we* value are threatened—by the imposition of a standardized assessment, by the creation of a curriculum in which we had little or no say, by conceptions of education and writing that we feel are dramatically different from our own. This would mean gathering the research-based best practices on which our work is based, seeking allies who concur with those positions and the values reflected in them, and then (eventually) engaging with—or even confronting—those who are challenging our values (and positions). While this approach can sometimes be valuable, it also has a very high cost, especially when the dominant frame currently shaping stories about education is so strong. The problem, of course, is that a values-based approach has very little room for strategic engagement or for compromise. On the other hand, it has enormous room for accommodating one's principles and values.

Issue-Based Alliance Building

Issue-based alliance building, finally, blends elements of interest- and values-based approaches to alliance building. Issue-based work is predicated on the idea that people will most *immediately* come together around their short-term interests; however, long-term social change will result only when these interests extend to and lead to action based on shared values. Issue-based organizing operates, then, along the boundaries of a three-sided triangle. On one side are individuals' passions as a starting point. As in interest-based work, the presumption here is that people can be inspired to action in and through these interests. For instance, Linda's neighbor was working to bring people together around their commitment to cheaper sidewalk repairs. But on the other side are values, which are seen as an important part of the change-making equation. The presumption here, as in a values-based approach, is that change can only happen when long-term values are affected, as well. In this model, Linda's neighbor might, then, use the opportunity to gather people around their commitment to less expensive repairs to open a dialogue focused on longer-term values associated with this passion—say, that commitment to citizen action described earlier, or the importance of equal access to city streets for people of all physical abilities, or any one of a number of issues that could be linked to sidewalks, neighbors coming together, or life in an urban neighborhood. From here, people would then identify longer-term projects they might want to work on that would represent those values, such as redefining urban space as public land. The connection between interests and values, then, forms the third side of the triangle.

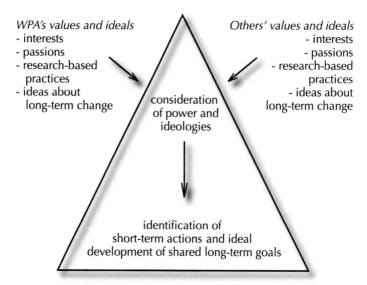

Fig. 1. Development of Platforms Based on Issues and Extending to Values and Interests

An issue-based approach blends elements of interest- and values-based work. Writing instructors or program directors working within an issue-based model certainly would identify their own values and principles, putting those on one side of a sort of conceptual triangle (see figure 1). Supporting these values would be both the instructor's or program director's interests and passions, as in interest-based work, and research-based practices that take into consideration long-term change, as in a values-based approach. Then she might also engage in dialogue with others, as in interest-based work, to hear about *their* passions and interests. But where an interest-based approach would suggest that the instructor, program director, writing center director, or department chair should focus on fostering others' capacity for change making, an issue-based approach would have the person consider questions of power and ideology wrapped up with these interests—her own, those associated with the interests of others, and so on. Then, she would navigate

among these different interests, along with their associated values and ideologies, to identify short-term, tactical actions that
might represent both her own interests (and values) and those
of potential allies. All the while, the instructor or program
director would also have an eye on the long-term, values-based,
implications of these actions and would make conscious decisions about how, when, and whether to take particular actions
with these bigger-picture strategic values in mind. In this sense,
the persona she might develop could reflect the principles
involved in what Cornel West (1989) calls "prophetic pragmatism," with its fundamental faith in the power of individuals to
make change, its belief in the never-perfect nature of American
democracy, *and* its acknowledgement of the unequal power relationships inherent in both processes for change making and
results of those processes.

When it comes to building alliances necessary to change stories and reframe assessment, it's hard to imagine not blending
elements from each of these approaches. That's because, as
Alinsky (1946) said of organizations, any instructor who wants
to reframe writing assessment needs to be nimble. We need to
find out about others' passions and interests and goals. But to
take the position that facilitation is our only, or even primary,
interest is to lose sight of the larger issues that underscore discussions about writing instruction and assessment, like the ones
illustrated by the different assessment questions raised by the
retention consultant on Linda's campus and the members of
her program. The questions we raise about these issues—and
our positions on them—are integrally bound with our own personal values, as well as the values of our field of composition
and rhetoric as they are reflected in best-practice principles like
those in position statements developed by the National Council
of Teachers of English (NCTE), the Conference on College
Composition and Communication (CCCC), or the Council of
Writing Program Administrators (CWPA).

We also need to remember that assessment questions and
methods raised by others that don't seem to jibe with our

interests and/or values are underscored by *their* values and
interests—and those might not necessarily align with ours. At
the same time, we need to be mindful that these values may not
be immediately visible or accessible to others. And so we need
to consider how we might build on short-term interests—those
shared passions—to develop or access long-term values. If we
cannot build to long-term change, are these projects still valuable? Or are short-term gains not worth the long-term costs?

Both of us, along with our colleagues Michele Eodice and
Joe Janangelo, recently had an experience in which we wrestled with questions like these. When the Common Core State
Standards Initiative (an effort involving Achieve, ACT, the
College Board, and others, working in conjunction with the
National Governors' Association) released standards intended
to represent what high school students needed to know to be
"prepared for college and career," the four of us—along with
many other professional colleagues—found the writing standards narrow and reductive. Discussions with others on a professional listserv led us to believe that the only position from
which we could have a hope of affecting these standards while
still in draft form (a window of about one month) was to speak
as "college writing experts" and say that these standards might
get students *into* college but that, from our positions as experts
on persistence and retention, we did not believe they would support students' success as they moved *through* college.

Since all of us are strongly committed to working with secondary (and elementary) colleagues *as* colleagues, envisioning
students' development as language learners throughout a K–16
(and beyond) education, none of us were comfortable taking
this position—yet, for the short-term possibility of potentially
influencing the standards, we did so. As we worked on this, we
also each provided our individual responses to the draft (and
Peggy even participated in providing feedback about the standards through her state's department of education, which had
asked her to review the *Common Core State Standards* as a content expert). This activity represented an instance in which

we collectively worked from a short-term persona—that of the "expert"—that was not at all comfortable for us. It didn't represent our short- or long-term interests. We did so, though, because we wanted to try to affect a larger issue that did represent our long-term interests and values (and the interests of students and teachers) that did represent those values, and we became convinced that we needed to adopt this collective personae to do so. Ultimately, these questions of trade-offs and short- and long-term gains are ones we can't answer for anyone but ourselves and our programs—but they crucial to consider.

THE ORGANIZING PERSONAE: ORGANIZING WORK, EMPLOYMENT STATUS, AND SOME ADDITIONAL IMPLICATIONS TO CONSIDER

As these summaries of approaches to forming alliances suggest, each requires the person who wishes to *do* some reframing—a faculty member, program director, or instructor—to step outside of roles that might be seen as traditionally associated with academe. As we described in chapters two and three, these roles are also bound up in very real ways with the same narratives currently dominating stories about education. Here, too, it's important to remember the lesson of chapters two and three: we must operate within the larger frames surrounding the academy and education more generally if we are to be understood as "legitimate."

Just as there are stories within these frames about what education should do (cultivate in citizens the ability to develop and the means to reach established ends), there are also stories about the role of the college or university faculty member in this process and, in fact, the development of the democracy to which this process is related (see Adler-Kassner 2010). This role, as historians James Carey (1978) and Thomas Bender (1993) have noted, is tightly bound up with the instantiation of the idea of the university as a "professional" training ground that evolved (not surprisingly) during the period around the turn of the nineteenth to the twentieth century. As new ideas and values entered the country (along with the millions of immigrants arriving during this period) and members of the dominant culture sought to create structures that would naturalize and "protect" values they saw as inherently "American," the movement to discipline-based professionalism described in chapter three led, among other things, to the primacy of specific disciplinary knowledge and methods distinctly separate from "politics." "[T]he authority of the professions" in this university, Carey notes, "was . . . derived from their presumed capacity to speak with the voice of positive science: to ground both their methods of selection and their understanding of human problems in the special methods and insight of science" (1978, 849).

The roles expected of twenty-first-century faculty members grow directly out of this nineteenth-century model. Recently, in fact, two well-respected, influential scholars in composition, Richard Haswell (2005) and Chris Anson (2008), have called in separate articles for writing researchers to attend to the tenets inherent in this kind of professionalism to ensure that the research that we conduct falls within the boundaries of empirical research. Anson contends that, in the face of critiques of some of writing instruction's most fundamental tenets (like the idea that grammar is best learned in context), compositionists might engage in "all forms of research, especially quantitative, . . . to pursue questions relevant to WPAs and their stewardship of successful writing programs, questions focusing especially on the nature of learning and the most supportable instructional methods and approaches" (23). It is important to make clear here that we *absolutely* agree with Anson's analysis, and we support the argument that he advances, along with Haswell (2005a), Russel Durst (1999), Richard Fulkerson (2005), Cindy Johanek (2000), and others, that it is absolutely essential for writing instructors to engage in empirical research involving a variety of methodologies. This research can help us understand what is actually going on in our classes and programs (rather than relying on our "felt sense" of students' and instructors' experiences).

When we enter into discussions about reframing writing assessment with allies on and off our campuses, though, we would do well to consider this very powerful story within the culture about what it means to *be* a faculty member. Anson calls for a shift away from "fighting belief with belief, conviction with conviction, theory with theory" and insists that we must "revive and reenergize" the empirical research agenda that "helped to create the field of composition" (2008, 32). This push for evidence-based research, rather than emotion-grounded action, is deeply embedded in guidelines for tenure and promotion; it also affects how college and university instructors are perceived outside and inside the classroom. But Kristine Hansen and others have noted that it sometimes implies a painful separation between personal convictions, often labeled "private," and public action (2005, 27–28; see also Elbow 2000, O'Reilley 2005, and Palmer 1998 on their perceptions of the problematic separation between personal convictions and "objective" research). Striking a balance between the expectations of postsecondary professionals (and the history of those expectations) and a desire to advocate for instructional practices (and the instructors and students who are implied in any discussion of those practices), then, is something that must be navigated in efforts to reframe writing instruction.

One of the ways to satisfy both the need for more empirical research and the call for assessment, as O'Neill, Schendel, and Huot explain, is positioning "assessment as research, as a way to ask and answer questions about our students, their writing, our teaching, our curricula and other factors" that comprise our teaching (2002, 14). Using research as a way to frame writing assessment encourages instructors and program directors to use their knowledge and skill as researchers in conducting assessments, contributing to disciplinary knowledge as well as to the validation argument needed for assessment. By following empirical research protocols—including both qualitative and quantitative methods—we can also move assessment from an administrative task to a disciplinary one, fulfilling our role as faculty members and not as managers. Using research to frame writing assessment is important because research is linked to disciplinary identity and the problems—or scope—of a field. By framing writing assessment as research, we have the potential not just to draw on our research expertise but also to influence how our field is defined.[1]

The persona that a writing instructor or program director chooses to adopt for reframing work could—and should—be seen as an effort to extend a more empirically sound, methodologically consistent, and intellectually grounded approach to assessment than is present in many of the options currently available (Adler-Kassner 2010). At the same time, it *might* be seen as an effort to "engag[e] the public, not merely inform it, [to] . . . participate in, and not remain detached from, efforts to improve the quality of public discourse [and] . . . understand . . . democracy as a way of life and not merely as a form of government" (Carey 1997, 207). This is not the researcher working at a distance, but one who sees her role as connecting with and advocating for particular approaches, ideas, and even ideologies. Choosing to occupy this persona, too, is a choice—and just as choosing among different approaches to building alliances, this choice comes with short- and long-term challenges and opportunities that writing instructors who want to reframe assessment should consider.

COMMUNICATING WITH STAKEHOLDERS: SHARING OUR STORIES

While decisions we make about how to build alliances and what personae we want to adopt in that process are important, none of the work we do in and through that process is useful if we don't communicate about it with others who are also interested

---

1. Huot and Neal (2006) argue specifically that writing assessment has been framed by concerns about reliability. This frame determines how researchers and practitioners conceive of writing assessment and develop methods. Their argument is more situated and focused, while we are addressing the framing of writing assessment more broadly.

in writing assessment. The importance of communication—of putting together stories, of creating messages from those stories, and of using those messages to compel and propel action around those stories—is reiterated in frame theory, as well as in values- and issue-based approaches to alliance building.

As people who spend our (work and, often, nonwork) lives thinking about language, it might be tempting to think we have a handle on this part of the process. But Joseph Harris, Dennis Baron, Mike Rose, and other composition researchers who have either scrutinized the ways writing instructors engage with audiences outside the academy and/or have engaged these audiences themselves have noted, we are notoriously inexperienced with this work. We can, of course, use theory from our own field to frame the issue, but we must remember (as rhetorical theory reminds us) the roles of audience, purpose, and context in shaping the message. However, as Rose notes, most of us are not necessarily accustomed to creating texts about our academic work for nonacademic audiences (2010). In fact, to succeed in graduate school (and beyond, for tenure and promotion), we must become comfortable and fluent in the language associated with rhetoric, writing, and composition studies, not one associated with broader audiences. This language is reflected and perpetuated in professional publications—our journals, books like this one, and so on. As we become immersed in this register, we perhaps begin to see it as "natural," at least when discussing composition research and related issues. But read any newspaper or magazine, listen to any discussion about writing, and it's easy to see how the language of composition, like all others, reflects the values of our profession and discourse communities.

Those of us who have attempted to write for audiences outside our disciplinary circle quickly realize that developing messages isn't a straightforward or simplistic process. In fact, the first mistake many advocates make is that they try to write a message—a slogan, an ad, or another piece of communication—without first clarifying just what that message is. In fact, these messages—these stories—are built in layers, through communication. Lakoff says that communication begins from deep frames, "moral values and principles that cut across issues and that are required before any slogans of clever phrases can resonate with the public" (2006, xii). Argument frames, which reflect the values of deep frames and are used to shape discussions across multiple issues, are layered on top of these. Next come surface frames (also sometimes called "spin"), positions on issues represented by people or groups (124–125). The last stage in the process is the creation of messages (36). Since these are constructed within genres, and since genres themselves outline roles for individuals and groups who participate in them (e.g., Bawarshi 2003; Bazerman 2004; Miller 1991), they also reflect the values and ideologies of the previous layers.

With all of this in mind, accessible strategies are important for developing and communicating messages about writing assessment. First, act locally. It's tempting, in the face of discussions about writing assessments that come from national groups like the Spellings Commission or national organizations like AAC&U, to jump into that bigger discussion by focusing on larger issues at play in the same broad, general terms as the policy reports quoted in chapters two and three. But as we've tried to demonstrate here, reframing writing assessment begins with building alliances and developing (and sharing) stories about our work at the *local* level—in our classes, programs, writing centers, departments, or campuses. When two- and four-year college writing teachers from around the country attended regional meetings on the Spellings Report held by the U.S. Department of Education (DOE), for instance, they told "stories of us" that addressed a concern shared by the DOE, the institutions at which these instructors taught, and the instructors themselves—improving student learning. Their stories described how they were addressing this concern through *local* assessment projects they had undertaken on their campuses. Grounding their contributions in this *national* discussion in vivid and specific *local* details made a difference—reports returned to the teachers suggested that the DOE representatives felt they had learned that writing teachers were taking the need for "accountability" seriously (Adler-Kassner 2008).

Second, carefully attend to language to create a shared vocabulary. To develop shared language that can shape our work with writing assessment, we need to listen carefully to the concerns people express, inside and outside our programs, about student learning and how they articulate those concerns. What constitutes "knowing" about student learning? What's considered acceptable evidence of that "knowing," and why? Sometimes we might use common words to describe a concern—"grammar" is a great example—but we might mean very different things. Faculty colleagues can tend to use "grammar" as a catch phrase for "anything I don't like about students' writing," from content to incorporation of evidence to syntax, whereas we mean something very specific. Other times, we use different language but are trying to convey the same ideas. Learning about how people describe "good writing" (or its inverse), and maybe even working with them to think carefully about what is embedded in assumptions about learning, can be important parts of accessing this shared vocabulary. From this shared vocabulary, it becomes easier to move to other issues that are integral parts of any assessment process, such as what each part considers evidence of achievement at various levels, how that achievement is demonstrated, and how it might be assessed. At the same time, there are important considerations here. In the example of the Spellings hearings, for instance, we mentioned that DOE representatives found writing instructors' stories of locally based assessments spoke to some concerns about "accountability." But while this term dominates discussions of assessment, it is not one we are comfortable using because it reflects a punitive, business-oriented approach that represents exactly what we are attempting to change through our efforts to reframe writing assessment—a different story, and not one in which we can participate (see Green 2009; Adler-Kassner and Harrington n.d.).

Only after working through these conceptual issues should writing instructors or program directors who want to reframe writing assessment begin to develop messages they want to advance through reframing efforts. Without this preliminary work, we risk communicating assumptions and positions that are not only inaccurate but that can be contradictory or, even worse, that can reinforce the very story we are trying to change. In actually crafting the message, however, instructors or program directors must be sure the texts communicate what those involved in the assessment *do* believe and *do* value (not what they don't).

For academics who are accustomed to writing long—long sentences, long paragraphs, long words—creating these messages can sometimes be challenging. (As Linda and one of her other writing partners often joke, "Why use twelve words when fourteen will do just as well?") But they need to be snappy and to the point. One of our favorite heuristic activities for creating these messages is to try to make bumper stickers for them— we literally give groups with whom we work paper the size of an average bumper sticker (about eight inches long by three inches wide) and tell them they need to distill the message they want to communicate through their assessment onto that space, and it must be visible from twelve feet away. These messages should be positive, communicating what they *do want*, not what they *don't*. The tag line "Writing Makes Things Happen" or "Writing is Everybody's Business, So Teach Your Writers Well" or "Write for Change" might represent some possible illustrations. Like other aspects of our processes and messages, these pieces also should reflect best-practice principles outlined in composition and rhetoric research (e.g., *CCCC Assessment Statement*; NCTE-WPA's *White Paper on Writing Assessment*). Media activist Robert Bray recommends "the brother-in-law test" for these messages—pick someone who isn't "associated with your cause or organization [like a brother-in-law], and see if they understand your issue" (2000, 16).

Finally, of course, it's important to disseminate the messages created about assessment processes and results. Writing instructors and program directors often find themselves in a reactive position when it comes to assessment—someone says we are (or aren't) doing something, and we need to respond. But we can also be proactive about sharing our ideas. Here, too, it's possible to work through a process. First, develop a communication plan. We can ask familiar questions: What audiences might be interested in hearing about your plan, and for what purposes? How can you communicate your values and ideas (clearly, concisely, and conceivably) to them? Engaging in assessment can help stakeholders outside the writing program understand and contribute to the values reflected in the program as well. Consider using a chart like the one in figure 2, for instance:

Message	Where	By Whom	When	Audience

Fig. 2. Communication Plan Matrix

Then, consider the best venue. Here, too, thinking and acting locally is key. Internal media—office newsletters, campus newspapers, even campus events—can be effective sites for sharing with others how an instructor or program is using valid, reliable, and discipline-appropriate assessment to improve student learning. Of course, it's always tempting (and can be quite satisfying) to send a letter or an opinion editorial (op-ed) piece to a local newspaper, too. Also, think about pitching a story to a local radio station (especially if the campus has a National Public Radio affiliate). Campus public relations offices also often welcome stories about events or activities in programs. If the writing program has something like a Celebration of Student Writing or other writing-related activity, be sure to let them know.

In all of these cases, remember general tips for clear communication with the media:

- Get to the point. News items are concise and direct, not long-winded and obtuse.

- Link your point to an ongoing story or trend. Media activists note that "three is a trend."

- Include specific examples. Stories about real people encountering real situations are powerful. This is also another reason we can be more effective at the local level: if you can localize a national story, you're more likely to get attention from local people (from administrators to journalists).

- Communicate what you *want* to happen, not what you don't want to happen. Trying to negate a message will only reinforce the original message (not the one you want to communicate) in the audience's minds.

- Stick to the message once it is developed. This may mean repeating it more times than you think is necessary, but remember—we're trying to change stories that are dominant in part because people hear them again and again.

- Check the media outlet's guidelines. Whether writing a letter or an op-ed piece, check the publication's requirements (which are typically included on the op-ed page). Letters and op-eds have word limits, and both are subject to editorial discretion. If they are edited, you won't be consulted about what is cut or kept, so make sure that your piece says what you want it to. If you're writing for a newspaper, consider using the inverted pyramid style for the piece. Put the most important thing, the message that you want to convey (not the one you want to negate!) at the beginning, the most important evidence about that message next, and so on.

- Develop relationships with the media you are most likely to use. If you want to write an op-ed piece, try to contact the op-ed editor with a query about the piece before sending. Introduce yourself, tell her or him what you would like to write about, and find out whether the paper would welcome such a contribution. If they would, ask about page limits and deadlines. Op-ed pieces can be sent to more than one paper; however, you do *not* want to send them to more than one outlet in the same market.

- As with all encounters with journalists, be *prepared* and *polite.* This could be the beginning of an ongoing relationship with this person, and you want to set the right tone. If you are trying to get an issue covered, consider contacting the reporter most likely to cover it, sending a press release, or both. Over time, this can provide a positive working relationship with the local press (Council of Writing Program Administrators Gallery 2008).

Using these strategies, coupled with smart assessment practices, we can reframe discussions about teaching and learning; we can highlight what we know and how we are continuously using valid, reliable, and discipline-appropriate assessment to improve teaching and learning. In the next chapter we look at reframing in action through brief case studies of instructors, program directors, and department chairs dealing with real-world writing assessment challenges.

5
REFRAMING IN ACTION

So far, we have been discussing the issue of reframing writing assessment through historical and theoretical lenses, and describing some processes writing instructors might use for reframing. In this chapter, we move away from abstract discussions to examine how reframing works in the complexity and messiness of the real world. We offer examples of real writing instructors and program coordinators working in real institutions under the real constraints we all experience. While we have selected these case studies purposefully to showcase successful, positive reframing efforts, we also acknowledge that these are not "ideal" or "perfect" models of reframing. (We discuss some of the complexities of reframing in chapter six, as well.) After all, most of us are not living in ideal worlds but rather the messier, more difficult and challenging conditions of higher education in the early twenty-first century. We have also selected different types of writing programs (i.e., first-year, writing center, and writing across the curriculum) and different types of institutions (i.e., two-year college, public comprehensive, and private liberal-arts-focused comprehensive) so readers can see how strategies, techniques, and challenges play out in different sites.

In all of these cases—some from our own original research and others from the published literature—the writing instructors, program directors, writing center directors, or department heads doing the assessment work didn't use the terminology of reframing we offer but rather explained or described their efforts in terms of trying to get something done in their postsecondary institutions. We highlight the way their work illustrates our claims and, at times, offer suggestions on ways they might have used other techniques or strategies. These suggestions are not offered as a statement of value of the instructor's or director's efforts or effectiveness, though—we aren't second-guessing them because we realize that working in real time is fraught with many more issues and problems than we can convey here. Instead, we offer our feedback for readers to help make connections between the case studies and the reframing theory and strategies we present.

FIRST-YEAR COMPOSITION PORTFOLIOS

As we discussed in chapter three, portfolios have been championed by college compositionists as a way of encouraging effective pedagogy while also satisfying demands for external assessment since Peter Elbow and Pat Belanoff's early articles about the portfolio assessment they developed at SUNY Stony Brook (Belanoff and Elbow 1986; Elbow and Belanoff 1986a, 1986b). In these essays, they describe how they used a portfolio of student writing produced as part of the composition course to replace the proficiency test, an impromptu essay exam, required by the university. The portfolio assessment, according to Elbow and Belanoff, "encourages good teaching and a sound writing process" (1986, 337). Students select their best writing from the course and have the benefit of drafting, receiving feedback, and revising their writing before submitting the portfolio, resulting in incentive to do better work. The Stony Brook portfolio system, Elbow and Belanoff argue, also encourages "collaboration among teachers" because it requires that instructors discuss the evaluation of sample papers and then participate in evaluating each others' portfolios as part of a team of evaluators (1986, 338). The portfolio system, they conclude, develops community standards for the writing program (339).

Compositionists have found Elbow and Belanoff's arguments convincing and have embraced writing portfolios for a variety of assessment purposes, whether in the classroom or beyond it, for placement, proficiency, and program assessment. In the process, these administrator -and/or teacher-researchers

have produced a prolific body of literature about writing portfolios. Portfolios are now commonly used in a variety of situations for outcomes-based assessment (again, in the classroom
and beyond). In the following two case studies, we look at first-
year composition program assessments that use student writing
portfolios. In each, the directors of the assessments respond
to local conditions as they navigate the challenges and opportunities provided by the assessment to improve teaching and
learning. We highlight these case studies, collected through
reviewing program materials and interviewing the writing program directors, to illustrate recent approaches to portfolios for
program assessment.[1]

Case Study 1: Introducing Portfolio Assessment at a Community College

At this two-year college, which we call Seaside Community
College,[2] the English department needed to create outcomes
and develop an assessment process to evaluate student learning
in light of the regional accreditation requirements. Located in
a historically rural but increasingly suburban county, students
at Seaside are required to take two writing courses: English
101, which focuses on critical reading, thinking, and writing;
and English 102, a writing intensive introduction to literature
course. There is also an advanced composition course, English
103, that students in the college honors program take in place
of 101, as well as three basic writing courses taught outside
the English department. Students are initially screened using
ACCUPLACER, a computer-adaptive, multiple-choice test. A

---

1. Although there are many cases of first-year composition proficiency portfolios in the literature, we offer two new case studies here to illustrate how
   portfolios have been adopted in the current higher education climate. In
   addition, by collecting our own case studies, we have been able to get a
   snapshot of the portfolio system in action, focus on our purposes, and get a
   sense of portfolio assessment as it has become more of a mainstream method
   of program assessment.

2. In this case study and others, we have used pseudonyms for individuals and
   institutions as indicated in our Human Subjects Review materials. All infor-
   mants gave informed consent prior to participation.

timed, impromptu essay, evaluated by writing faculty, determines final placement for students whose ACCUPLACER scores
are low. Professor Murphy, now chair of the English department[3], notes that the essay is the most important factor in determining the students' placement; some are moved up to 101 and
some are moved down to a developmental course.

As part of the final assessment in both English 101/103 and
102, students compile a writing portfolio. The portfolio consists
of a preliminary self-reflection, the placement essay, all graded
essays for the course, workshop activities (often focused on isolated writing skills), and a final course reflection. English 102
students continue the same pattern—completing the portfolio
with all graded essays, workshop activities, and a final portfolio
self-critique. The portfolios serve two purposes: for the class,
they are graded and contribute to the students' final course
grades in lieu of a final exam; for the program, they are evaluated as direct evidence for ongoing outcomes-based assessment.

For program assessment, faculty review every third portfolio
in their class (based on a roster) using a common checklist. Each
year the checklist varies according to what course outcomes the
department has decided to highlight. Thirteen objectives were
specified for the writing courses when the assessment was first
developed. Each year the department identifies a subset of these
for the assessment. In the five years since the portfolio assessment
was initiated, twelve of the initial thirteen outcomes have been
addressed in the portfolio assessment. Although faculty members
are only required to complete the checklist for the assessment,
according to Professor Murphy, most also include discursive comments. Professor Murphy compiles the checklist results, writes
an annual assessment report, submits it to the administration,
and shares it with her colleagues in the English department. At
the department level, the report, as well as the informal written

---

3. At Seaside, as at many community colleges, there is no designated writing
   program administrator per se. Faculty teach courses in composition and
   literature, and the responsibility of coordinating writing courses falls to the
   department chair.

feedback, is used as the basis for department discussions about curriculum, pedagogy, and plans for the next academic year.

Professor Murphy reports that before the portfolio assessment was developed, some faculty members and administrators understood writing as a complex, meaning-making activity, but many were more focused on issues of grammar, mechanics, and usage. This view had been reflected in the institution's assessment practices. At the college level, in response to the pressure for evidence of student learning, students' writing practices had been assessed using a multiple-choice exam that included no actual writing. Professor Murphy, who took several composition and rhetoric courses while earning her MFA, saw a need for an assessment grounded in the principles of that discipline and based on authentic course artifacts. She also saw that this need for more discipline-based assessment could be an opportunity to make some changes around instruction and assessment in the program as well, especially in two key areas. First, Professor Murphy saw that instructors were dissatisfied with workload distribution in the English department. Some instructors taught regular 101 courses, while others taught 101R, a five-credit version of the same course that included a "review," but purported to address the same outcomes. Second, she saw a chance to address concerns over the curriculum, which some instructors wanted to shift toward an inquiry- and content-based model from one that focused more on form. Professor Murphy saw an opportunity in the institution's need for assessment and decided to investigate programmatic uses of portfolios as well as outcomes-based composition programs in other institutions. Ultimately, she led the English department's effort to design a new assessment, which resulted in the portfolio process described above.

Professor Murphy, who at that time was not the department chair but a department faculty member, explains that in designing the portfolio evaluation system, she ignored the multiple-choice test being used at the institutional level and "simply went about my research and design, quietly meeting with the English department" to learn more about what her departmental colleagues valued in student writing. In the process, she also learned about colleagues' interests and how those interests were reflected in teaching and student work. As a result of these discussions, she learned that in her small department, four of the six department members were very supportive of the shift to portfolio-based assessment—the two who were not "wanted to leave the old system in place." The college administration, however, was very supportive of her work because politically it needed a department "that was taking outcomes seriously" and wanted "a model for outcomes-based assessment."

Because the portfolio resulted in a curricular change—the elimination of 101R and the change in credit hours for 101— Professor Murphy also had to gain support of the college's Academic Council. She explains that she met with every group on campus she could and just kept repeating her message about the value of the portfolio in the classroom in promoting best practices in teaching, and about the value of assessment in providing direct evidence of student learning. She also argued— and demonstrated through assessment findings—that there was no real change in the credit hours being taught by the English faculty but that the hours would be more evenly distributed across faculty with the elimination of 101R. By working with administrators' interests in creating a useful assessment, faculty colleagues' interests in redistributing workload, and the Academic Council's interests in curricular and equity issues, Professor Murphy was able to change the discussion about not only assessment, but also instruction, in her department.

But while Professor Murphy has been able to reframe assessment toward practices that more closely reflect the values she brings based on her work as a teacher and a professional well-versed in best practices, she is still frustrated by the college administration's need for easily reported statistics, which are generated by the checklists faculty use as they assess portfolios:

> Because our college needs statistics, I've never really had the opportunity to look at completed portfolios like a researcher. I feel more

like a statistician. The statistics satisfy a bureaucratic purpose, but I originally wanted to examine the writing in a fashion similar to that of Anne Herrington and Marcia Curtis in *Persons in Process*. The challenge is time and bureaucracy. The institution needs numbers for reports, and our teaching load is so heavy that I doubt anyone will have the time to simply study the evidence.

Professor Murphy would like to be able to do more in-depth analysis of the portfolios—or even of a subset of them—and do a qualitative, longitudinal study of students' development as writers. In other words, she currently sees the portfolios framed by an administrative function, but she would like to reframe them—at least in part—as a disciplinary activity. However, she notes that the high teaching load and demand for service at her community college has made it impossible for her to engage in formal disciplinary research beyond what she already has conducted. At the same time, while Professor Murphy has not been able to delve as deeply into the writing portfolios as she would like, she admits that "the statistics provide some faculty with data to support their understanding of our student population." The portfolio assessment, she adds, also has created a positive understanding about the composition program across campus: "It's commonly understood that we manage to teach, fairly effectively, essay structure, constructing an arguable thesis statement, gathering and using evidence (research), and addressing different audiences." On the other hand, she notes that many of their students "struggle (and continue to struggle) with sentence structure."

Professor Murphy also identifies additional benefits that have accrued as a result of the statistics she compiles, noting that "[t]he portfolio outcomes assessment [the statistics] have proven to be powerful in unifying a focus in the classroom among writing faculty." She illustrates how the program has used the results to improve classroom instruction:

> The first time we looked at how well our students follow MLA style, the results were humbling. [Based on the results], we—as a group— simply focused more time in the classroom on documentation and

stopped taking it for granted that students would figure it out themselves just because they had a handbook. [Additionally], one of our program goals is to teach the parts of the argument (introduction, background, partition, confirmation, refutation, and conclusion). Students seem to do well with all but "refutation." Recent statistics suggest that about half our English 101 students respond to opposing positions by refuting evidence, adjusting a position, or conceding a point. In the fall, we'll focus on this more in the classroom (and modify our assignments).

While Professor Murphy acknowledges the statistics as both problematic and beneficial, she finds that portfolio assessment has influenced both classroom teaching and the composition program as a whole in positive ways. Professor Murphy explains that based on the assessments, the English department revised the composition program goals from thirteen outcomes to just five. The portfolio assessment also provides a basis for ongoing, less formal discussions about teaching and learning across the department, according to Professor Murphy. Because the 102 portfolio contains work from the students' earlier course(s) as well as the placement exam, faculty get a sense of what is happening across the program. Another less tangible consequence of the English 102 portfolio assessment, according to Professor Murphy, is the faculty's appreciation for how students develop as writers from their initial placement essay through the end of the sequence: as a writing faculty, "we've come to love the comprehensive self-critique in English 102 . . . and it's fascinating to read how students respond to the change in their writing from the time they wrote that placement essay through the end of English 102."

Case Study 2: First-Year Composition Portfolios in a Comprehensive State University

Unlike the situation at Seaside Community College, the writing program director at this comprehensive state university inherited an established portfolio assessment program. As an

English faculty member at what we call Grand State University, Professor Bailey directs the first-year composition program and leads a yearly portfolio assessment of first-year student writing at her public comprehensive university. The comp program consists of three courses: one developmental (English 90) and two regular (English 101 and 102). Although Professor Bailey—who has a PhD in composition and rhetoric and had several years of experience before taking the position at Grand State—has only been directing the program for three years, the portfolio assessment has been in place for over ten. As part of the College of Arts and Sciences assessment plan, Grand State set aside a small budget to support assessment of core courses and let areas create their own assessment process. For many years, according to Professor Bailey, the yearly assessment was led by a full-time lecturer who received one course of reassigned time to collect portfolios, lead a two-day reading session, and write an assessment report. Based on the a process developed with Grand State's Institutional Research Office at that time, readers—instructors from within the first-year writing program—gathered to assess one "competency" (outcome) per year, across student work from all three first-year writing courses.

As she explains, Professor Bailey sees the portfolio assessment as "both an opportunity to see, across our program, what students do well and what we feel isn't being taught as consistently as we'd like, and it's a vital way for us to reconsider and revise our course content." Across the university, the competency-based portfolio assessment received accolades and was featured in a recent accreditation report, according to Professor Bailey, so there has been support for the work. Professor Bailey explains that because the assessment is based on a portfolio of work produced in a course, it has the potential to frame writing in ways consistent with the rhetorical, process-oriented approach that composition studies promotes and that is valued within the first-year writing program. However, she notes that there has also been some tension in this frame, or as she phrases it, "between the larger frame and the earlier use of the assessment," since the competency most frequently assessed in the past—and therefore featured in the reports—was often related to grammar, mechanics, and citation practices. These competencies, Professor Bailey explains, were often viewed as the most "reliably assessable."

In her first year as the program director, Professor Bailey (who was not yet tenured) began working with colleagues in the program to understand the assessment process and to initiate some revisions to it. She began by having "lots of committee meetings with a committed group of first-year comp instructors and any of the comp-rhet faculty who wanted to join in." Internally, she framed this process "as an opportunity to reacquaint ourselves with other professional models of assessment and to make the process more meaningful for us and our program." They discussed "what the one-competency model revealed—and all that it didn't" as well as reading some scholarship on assessment and from reading theory, focusing on "*how* we read, respond to, and engage with student writing." These discussions, she explains, were aimed at helping the portfolio reading team—and the instructors in the program—"read and assess the student work in a way that responded better to our field's [composition studies] understanding of writing assessment." The portfolio readers, according to Professor Bailey, learned about and discussed what it means to read and assess student work holistically, and they also wrestled with questions about reliability and reading theory. "Singling out competencies for assessment had inevitably made some aspects visible while leaving much of the reading experience invisible, and as a team they worked to rethink what it might mean to read student work differently." Along with these discussions, Professor Bailey also organized a workshop for the portfolio assessment committee with a national expert on assessing portfolios. Based on the workshop, according to Professor Bailey, that year's portfolio assessment committee "collaborated on a revised assessment process, creating new scoring guides and practicing with reading more holistically." As part of the revision, first-year writing program administrators agreed to reconfigure the assessment budget so there was additional money for more readers. Increasing the number of readers was important to her because she sees "this kind of assessment as an important part of professional development—for both brand-new instructors and for our long-time instructors."

Professor Bailey reports that throughout this process the portfolio assessment committee "talked at length about how our program assessment *matters*—first to us within the first-year comp program, because it helps us see potential areas for workshops and so on; but also on campus: how we talk about writing (and even how we *do* the assessment) in turn shapes how others see it. We wanted to represent student writing—and our reading of it—in a richer way." As the writing program director, Professor Bailey wanted the assessment to be "*clearly* tied to where the program is now and where we want to be going." In other words, she wanted the assessment to be more closely aligned with what the program espoused. So during the readings, the portfolio assessment committee collected more information on what they were reading and what they thought about what they read in the portfolios. The changes, then, included increasing the number of portfolios collected (currently three from each section of each first-year writing course); reading with new collaboratively designed, holistic scoring guides; identifying noteworthy student texts with sticky notes during the readings; and reflecting in discussions and written responses during the reading days. As Professor Bailey admits, "These discussions were very rich and informative—often as helpful, or more helpful, than the results from the portfolio reading itself, and the reflections became a key part of the assessment project that really helped push us forward. Within our program, then, we could frame how the assessment process was both an opportunity for professional development (through participating as a portfolio assessment committee member) *and* how the assessment process demonstrated what we needed to work on together." It created, in Professor Bailey's words, "a kind of collective agreement" which "was really, really important to be able to bring back to the larger group."

Based on this ongoing work, Professor Bailey explains how the current portfolio assessment model has built upon the foundation she inherited when she came into her position:

- Gather three portfolios from every section of all three first-year comp courses.

- Read and score portfolios holistically during a two-day stretch—portfolios are first read and scored by the classroom instructor and then by a portfolio assessment committee member (a version of the two-tiered scoring system). Score with a holistic rubric developed by our initial portfolios assessment committee—a rubric that was created from (1) an internal list of values for student writing generated by the committee; (2) the established outcomes (still called competencies, but hopefully not for much longer); and (3) the WPA *Outcomes Statement* (which was used a means of situating their work in the larger picture, but Professor Bailey reports that they won't be using it in the future since the program outcomes have been revised and are more closely aligned to the WPA *Outcomes Statement*).

- During the scoring, readers (1) mark "other factors that lead to this assessment." This portion of the scoring has proven instrumental in helping capture the ideas "beyond the rubric" (Broad 2003), including the classroom-context-sensitive reading of the instructor and the program-context-sensitive reading of the portfolio assessment committee team member; and (2) use sticky notes to mark innovative student work and/or interesting assignments.

- Each course is read together at one time (i.e., all portfolios for the developmental course are read and evaluated before moving on to 101 and then 102). After each class, readers (as a group) generate written reflections and have an open discussion on what they have seen,

enjoyed, and noticed. ("These discussions," reports
Professor Bailey, "have been crucial.")

At the end of this process, Professor Bailey drafts a report based
on the reading and results, and it is revised with input from
that year's portfolio assessment committee. The report shapes
their program directions for the year and also is shared with the
department chair, the dean, and others on campus.

While Professor Bailey finds this a productive process that
provides information for both external demands and internal
program use, she notes there are still challenges. The first is
that the current scoring guides are pulled from sources beyond
the program, which was done intentionally to increase the disciplinary substance of what the scoring guide aimed for. However,
according to Professor Bailey, "It sometimes made instructors
feel like they were aiming for two slightly different targets."
Additionally, the scoring guide prompts the reader first to determine if there is evidence that the course goal was addressed,
then to determine if the goal was achieved. After this, the reader
decides what level of proficiency was achieved in reference to
the particular goal: highly proficient, proficient, not proficient.
This guide, according to Professor Bailey, "gives us great general
information but not as much nuanced information. It's more
challenging to communicate what the scores 'mean' to those
beyond the first-year comp program." The second challenge,
according to Professor Bailey, is to increase participation in
the portfolio reading: "The same instructors often participate,
which undermines the professional development opportunities
for the program as a whole."

To address these challenges, Professor Bailey has continued
to work with the portfolio assessment committee to modify the
assessment in response to changes in the program, results from
the assessment, and other local factors. For example, having
revised the outcomes for the first-year composition program,
the committee is in the process of revising the scoring rubric
so it is more intentionally aligned with the outcomes. Professor

Bailey reports that they are also developing some more nuanced pilot projects associated with the portfolio readings such as focusing on the library requirement or the stretch program. She anticipates that these " 'close-up pictures,' will help supplement the macro lens view that the other reading/scoring" provides. She is "hopeful that others will participate. As it is, though, the people that come are really engaged and energetic—which is a great thing!"

Although Professor Bailey can identify symbiotic connections between the portfolio assessment and the first-year writing program, she is less able to see if the changes in the assessment—or the program—have had any impact campus-wide. In part, this is because the changes are relatively recent. She notes, however, that others "are pleased that we're doing assessment and that they can highlight it" and acknowledges that she "now need[s] to do a better job of meeting with key players and demonstrating what we're doing." As a relatively new faculty member—and an untenured one when she began at Grand State—Professor Bailey has concentrated on building alliances within her department and program. As she has become more established at Grand State, she realizes she needs to work beyond the department to build alliances across the institution.

ଓଃ

In both of the cases presented here, the writing faculty/program directors used their disciplinary knowledge to frame a portfolio assessment that not only satisfied the institution's need for outcomes assessment but also provided useful feedback for the writing program. They considered local contexts—such as program history, governing structures, faculty, and their own institutional positions—as they responded to institutional demands. Acting incrementally, these program directors considered the long term issues and goals in addition to immediate ones—Professor Murphy's desire to address issues around workload, for instance, or Professor Bailey's to address a wider range of course outcomes. As a result, the portfolio assessments are framed by disciplinary theories and values yet still responsive to the institutions' needs and context.

TRANSFORMING WAC THROUGH ASSESSMENT

Like first-year composition, writing across the curriculum (WAC), and related programs—such as writing in the disciplines (WID) and communication across the curriculum (CAC)-based programs—are frequent sites of assessment because they are typically tied directly to an institution's undergraduate learning outcomes. One important difference, though, is that WAC, WID, or CAC programs operate across departments and colleges. Their wider reach can create different challenges and opportunities than does a first-year writing program. Sometimes, professional accreditation agencies, such as those for engineering and business, are involved in WAC assessments because accrediting agencies include written communication standards for programs. Another difference in WAC-based programs that can influence assessment demands relates to funding—they may need to demonstrate their value (and assessment is a way to do that) to maintain funding (whether in-house funding or external grant funding) because they operate outside the department-based structure found in most colleges and universities.

In this section, we highlight two WAC-related assessment programs: one operates across departments as a creative response to regional accreditation demands, while the other is part of the College of Engineering, satisfying professional accreditation requirements from that college's disciplinary accrediting body. Both have been developed within the last ten years as accreditation agencies have moved to focus more on evidence of student learning. We begin with Seattle University's, which has been the topic of many conference presentations and several journal articles. (We do not use a pseudonym for Seattle University and its WAC specialist, John Bean, because there are several published reports about the program, and their efforts have been featured at many conferences. In fact, Seattle is a featured model on the Council of Writing Program Administrators' Assessment

Gallery. We draw on these sources and conversations with Professor Bean.)

Case Study Three: Discourse-Based Assessment in the Disciplines

John Bean, along with his colleagues at Seattle University, has used the demand for assessment that came from an accreditation review as the impetus to reframe and rejuvenate the writing-across-the-curriculum program at that institution. Seattle University is a private Catholic Jesuit institution, with 3,500 undergraduate students. The university, comprised of eight colleges, offers over sixty undergraduate programs and thirty graduate programs, with a full-time faculty of approximately 445 full-time and 218 part-time faculty. John Bean, a tenured Professor of English, currently serves as Seattle University's Consulting Professor of Writing and Assessment.

Seattle's "infusion model of WAC" began in 1986 "with the inauguration of a new core curriculum that mandated 'a significant amount of writing' in every core course" but without any designated writing intensive courses (Bean, Carrithers, and Earenfight 2005, 5). Bean was hired in the English department to provide faculty support and coordinate the WAC effort: "In the 80s and 90s, WAC received considerable attention on campus," one result of which was Bean's book *Engaging Ideas: The Professor's Guide to Integrating Writing, Critical Thinking, and Active Learning in the Classroom* (5). However, as in many WAC programs, after the initial workshops, "interest in WAC was maintained primarily by a small network of faculty who valued WAC's ongoing pedagogical conversations " (5). By the end of the 1990s, there was no discernible WAC program, according to Bean, Carrithers and Earenfight.

But as interest in WAC per se was waning, pressures for assessment were waxing. Seattle University's new strategic plan focused attention on assessment, and additional attention to assessment was coming from the regional accrediting body. Furthermore, the upper level administration "recogni[zed] that assessment—properly instituted—might have a positive impact on student learning and faculty development" (Bean, Carrithers, and Earenfight 2005, 6). Prior to this, the university had no comprehensive assessment plan, and "resistance to assessment was fierce in the arts and sciences, where many faculty protested the reductionism of standardized tests, the anticipated loss of classroom autonomy, the time demands that assessment seemed to impose, and the general philosophic positivism and corporate mentality that seemed to underlie the assessment movement" (6).

As part of an accreditation self-study, Seattle took what is often the first step toward assessment designed to improve teaching and learning, creating "for the first time—a list of learning outcomes for its undergraduate majors" (Bean, Carrithers, and Earenfight 2005, 6). Importantly, Bean, Carrithers, and Earenfight say, "almost every department included, as one of its outcome statements, the desire that graduating seniors be able to produce an apprentice professional paper within the discipline's discourse" (6). But while almost all departments stated this desire, few if any of the departments required that type of paper of all majors, and they had no assessment process in place to evaluate student performance. Given this situation, Seattle received "a 'revisit in five years' mandate" increasing "the pressure to create an assessment plan" (6).

As the university explored ways to respond not only to the need for assessment but also to faculty concerns about it, they invited consultant Barbara Walvoord, a well-known WAC scholar whose more recent work also includes assessment, to campus. Seattle adapted Walvoord's approach to learning outcomes assessment, creating a model whereby departmental faculty select a course assignment they feel addresses a particular outcome and embed it in a course. The student products resulting from the embedded assignment are then graded by the course instructor using a rubric. The instructor analyzes the rubric scores, seeking patterns of strengths and weaknesses that are then discussed with the whole department at a meeting devoted to assessment. Faculty discussion aims at finding ways to ameliorate weaknesses ("close the loop") through modifications in instructional methods, better assignment sequencing and scaffolding, or other means. These course-embedded assignments can be any type of product—an oral presentation, an essay, a research report, an exam, a multimedia project, or a painting. Because in practice "most of the products are papers or oral presentations," the "potential impact" on WAC was readily apparent to Bean and his colleagues who were already invested in WAC (Bean, Carrithers and Earenfight 2005, 6). This approach, aided by the long history of WAC at Seattle and by Bean's expertise as the WAC coordinator, built upon the faculty's innate interest in improving teaching and learning and in the validation it gave to instructors' grading of student performance as an assessment act. It also positioned Bean to take a lead role in implementing Walvoord's approach, which Seattle has termed "a discourse-based approach to assessment" based on the way it produces rich faculty talk about student learning as opposed to psychometric data requiring statistical analysis.

As Professor Bean continues to work with departments using this approach, we see him using strategies we described in chapter four. He begins by building alliances with individual departments and their faculty, learning what they find important about disciplinary ways of writing, thinking and knowing, and why. From this discussion, Bean then helps them (1) identify a learning outcome to focus on, (2) determine where in the curriculum that outcome is addressed (or demonstrated), (3) identify an assignment that showcases that learning outcome, (4) develop a rubric for evaluating the assignment, and (5) use the results as the basis for department reflection and discussion and, where appropriate, adjustments to teaching and/or curriculum. Each department writes an annual report that summarizes the results of the year's assessment project. The university assessment committee collates and compiles the individual reports for the college and university. Since implementing this plan, departments as diverse as history, English, chemistry, finance, and economics have embraced this approach and used it not only as a means to satisfy a mandate but also as the basis for curricular revision and faculty development. In addition, many have presented results of the assessment at professional conferences and in peer-reviewed journals (e.g., Alaimo, Bean, Langenhan, and Nichols, 2009; Bean, Carrithers and Earenfight 2005; Carrithers, Ling, and Bean 2008; Carrithers and Bean 2008). Professor Bean also successfully led a team of collaborators in obtaining two assessment grants from the Teagle Foundation, which connects the assessment work at Seattle with Gonzaga, a Jesuit university in Spokane.

Part of the success of Seattle's efforts was in the way Bean connected the assessment mandate with the WAC program. He built alliances with colleagues across campus around an issue that they felt strongly about—students' ability to write and think like disciplinary professionals—and used that initial issue to develop long-term partnerships that addressed the demand for assessment. Drawing on his experience with WAC, he framed the assessment mandate as a way to support faculty's efforts to promote more engaged student learning. He used the consulting approach from his WAC work to assist departmental faculty in satisfying the assessment in a way that fit their needs and respected their expertise. He also partnered with a nearby university to garner external funding for part of the work, which provided additional legitimacy for their efforts. It's important to point out here that this frame is affirming and positive—it's about building on what faculty already do—rather than being denigrating, negative, or directed toward proving something. Once faculty saw the benefits to their teaching, the department's major curriculum, and the students' learning, there was buy-in. The assessment, then, has provided a way for Bean to revitalize the discussions about the teaching and evaluation of writing, and actually extend the earlier work on writing in the Core to writing in the disciplines. Assessment data now being gathered permit observation of student writing from the first year through the Core and major. As part of these efforts, Professor Bean and his colleagues clearly articulated a theoretical framework for writing and shared it with faculty across the campus as well as in all of the documents the discourse-based assessment program generates.

Bean also encouraged faculty to see the assessment work as part of their scholarship, co-authoring publications with many of them. This kind of recognition helps communicate the value of the work to the administration (who by all accounts have been pleased with the efforts). For the disciplinary faculty leading the efforts, a peer-reviewed publication or conference presentation is tangible acknowledgement of the work they have done, making the assessment more than just "service." Securing external funding also validates the assessment work for Bean and the other faculty who participate.

In interviews and discussions, Professor Bean explains that although not all faculty resistance to assessment has been overcome, many now see the value of a discourse-based approach. While the work being done at Seattle has been recognized by the national community, Bean admits that he and his colleagues have been less effective about communicating its success on campus beyond certain constituencies (such as administrators and faculty already involved in the assessment). The administration is pleased with the work, but the larger university community has not always understood its value, explains Bean.

More recently, Bean has partnered with the director of the writing center to offer workshops in "writing in the major" (funded through the Teagle grant) to support departments' desire to create capstone projects for seniors and to use assessment efforts to promote the "backward design of the curriculum" in which scaffolded and sequenced assignments build on each other to teach disciplinary ways of conducting inquiry, using evidence, and making disciplinary arguments in conversation with the professional literature. Bean has continued to co-author articles and presentations with faculty from across the disciplines. Through building alliances on his campus, Bean reframed the demand for assessment into an opportunity to transform Seattle's WAC program by discussing writing theory and practices with faculty, developing a consensus across and within the disciplines about writing theory, pedagogy, and evaluation, and improving teaching and learning with locally developed and administered assessments.

Case Study Four: Building an Engineering Communication Assessment

While Seattle's WAC assessment includes, potentially, all department majors, this next case is more narrowly focused on an engineering program. The program director, an untenured assistant professor whom we call Professor Jones, administers the communication and professional development program in the College of Engineering as part of a larger institution we call State Tech University. Her undergraduate degree is in an engineering field, but her graduate work is in English and includes both literature and rhetoric and composition. She has held a variety of administrative and teaching positions in both English and professional communications. As part of her administrative responsibilities, she regularly conducts two assessments for the Accreditation Board for Engineering and Technology (ABET) accreditation that involve writing: (1) a biennial assessment of a subsample of students' communication portfolios against a subset of programmatic learning outcomes, and (2) an annual assessment of a stratified subsample of students' capstone portfolios (which include written and oral proposals, progress reports, and final reports) based on the student learning outcomes stipulated by ABET. The first, according to Professor Jones, is more strictly speaking a writing assessment while the second involves much more since only one of ABET's outcomes is "the ability to communicate effectively." In this narrative we focus on the biennial communication portfolio since it focuses more on writing.

The communication portfolio assessment requires all engineering students to take a senior level course in communication. The course has three specified learning outcomes, all connected to the portfolio:

1. Describe the development of their communication and collaboration skills over time, using graded work as evidence of skill level.

2. Explain the relationship between situation (audience, purpose, and context) and effectively designed communication (content, organization, visual design and representation, language, style) for a range of written and oral workplace documents.

3. Describe the process of producing documents and presentations collaboratively.

While all student portfolios are evaluated as part of the requirement for the course (in light of the specified course outcomes), the biennial program assessment uses these same portfolios. Professor Jones describes the biennial assessment process:

> Every other summer, a team of external evaluators assesses a purposive subsample of the communications portfolios completed as part of [the communication portfolio course]. The subsample is designed to include high, middle, and low-scoring students based on average grades across the ECP [Engineering Communication Program] curriculum. The evaluators are expert technical communications instructors; typically, they are university faculty who teach English XXX: Technical Writing, a course that serves students across the university (but not the course in which the portfolios are created).
>
> The evaluators score each portfolio using a rubric that addresses approximately one-third of the ECP outcomes; correctness and conciseness are addressed in each assessment; other outcomes are rotated to insure that over a six-year period, all outcomes are assessed. Each outcome is scored on a 5-point scale, with 1 as the lowest and 5 as the highest possible score (a score of 0 indicates the evaluator did not have enough information to assess the item; no scores of 0 were reported).
>
> To norm the evaluators, all three evaluators, along with the program directors and assistant director, read and score sample

portfolios. In any area where evaluators differ by more than one point, the evaluation team discusses the criteria and reaches a consensus regarding scoring standards.

All portfolios in the sample are then scored by two evaluators and the scores averaged. If the two evaluators differ by more than one point on more than one question, the portfolio is scored by the third evaluator, and all three scores are averaged.

Professor Jones explains that as she initiated this assessment at her institution, the frames surrounding writing—and writing assessment—at her institution as a whole were shifting. Previously, State Tech's engineering students were required to take two writing intensive (WI) courses, with WI "defined by number of pages written and inclusion of revision." As part of this shift, though, a more broad-based communication requirement in which students across departments would compile a portfolio that included writing, speaking, and visual texts, but in which the specific texts would be defined by each department, was being implemented. No one wanted to talk particularly about assessment, though each department's new communication plan had to include assessment to be approved. She concludes, "So I suppose at one level, the institution didn't frame writing and writing assessment at all or in anything like concrete terms."

But while the university may not have explicitly articulated its frames, the early WI requirement did frame writing in particular ways: writing was important for all students; certain upper level courses were considered WI (and others, presumably, were not expected to promote writing in the same ways). Professor Jones also explains that there were some common criteria—or expectations—across the university for these courses: fifteen pages of graded writing and opportunities for revision. It seems that assessment of writing was not directly addressed in any serious way beyond the course grades in this type of program. Students taking and passing the individual courses were deemed to have satisfied the requirement. Faculty members were provided with little if any support. She continues explaining that at around the same time, the university had only just completed its first writing assessment, which was led by English faculty, focused on first-year composition, and was conducted by the first-year composition director. Professor Jones participated in this assessment as one of the scorers.

Although the university as a whole had not been very concerned with assessment, Professor Jones explains that the College of Engineering was regularly involved with assessment because of ABET. In 2000, ABET revised its assessment criteria and introduced Engineering Criteria 2000, which Professor Jones describes as "a huge shift for ABET, moving from a bean counting approach (x many credit hours in area a, x many in b, etc.) to an outcomes-based approach in terms of student learning. Frankly," she says, "no one really knew what do with any of the outcomes, so the 'framing' of writing assessment—communication, actually—was pretty vague and confusing." As she began the portfolio assessment in 2003, "the college had only recently gone through its first round of ABET reviews under EC2000." Professor Jones says that although there didn't seem to be a clear understanding about writing (or communication) or the assessment of it in EC2000 or in the college, the pressure was definitely there. Assessment had to be done "regularly because ABET accreditation occurs every six years, so assessment is a continual part of most departments' operations. Not necessarily a pleasant part, or something that is used effectively, but always there." Additionally, because of this new requirement from ABET, she explains, "All new course proposals in the college have to include documentation showing which of the ABET learning outcomes the course meets, for example. And many departments have paperwork in place designed to be linked to continuous assessment. Some are better than others at linking assessment to improvement."

In designing the communication portfolio assessment, Professor Jones was influenced in part by the ABET requirements because ABET was a key stakeholder; however, she drew more directly on "what I knew about writing program administration and assessment to create and shape the approach." As part of the English department, she had participated in the assessment of the first-year program and the university-wide writing program, both of which led her to learn more about the theory and practice of writing assessment. Because of the institution's "limited and abstract framework and (now) departmentally controlled" approach, Professor Jones explains that she "had a great deal of freedom to develop assessments" that she "thought were productive. Satisfying ABET was the only institutional concern. Everything else emerges from my disciplinary knowledge in technical communication [communication in the disciplines] and engineering education." For example, Professor Jones describes how the use of portfolios in her classroom (which encourages students to revise, reflect, and take ownership of their work) influenced her approach to the program assessments. She also notes that she paid more attention to assessment when it was addressed in disciplinary contexts, such as attending conference presentations and reading journal articles and books.

When she took over the program, "there was no regular assessment of any sort. Although the writing portfolio did exist," it was "less of a portfolio than a collection of graded work from classes across three years, and it was limited in the information it provided." She explains that it seemed "quite crazy to direct a writing program that didn't have assessment, based on everything [she] knew about programs and administration and the need for regular assessment. So [she] created the writing portfolio assessment first." Over time, Professor Jones explains, she has "made continual changes to the writing portfolio to create a better representation of student work, including adding reflective components, requiring students to describe the artifacts included, providing a greater degree of choice and flexibility in selecting artifacts, and shifting the entire framework from a 'writing portfolio' to a 'professional portfolio.' The artifacts are still texts, and thus can be used for programmatic assessment, but the portfolio is slowly gaining more value for students."

Professor Jones reports many benefits of the portfolio assessment, aside from "passing" the most recent ABET accreditation (which included far more than the portfolio assessment she administers). "The most significant effects" of the assessment, according to Professor Jones, "have been in terms of ongoing program development that dovetails with a wholesale programmatic shift from format-centered instruction to a more audience/activity system/rhetorical-centered approach along with paradigmatic shifts in the conception of engineering education nationally." She elaborates on the specifics of these benefits, explaining that the

> list is fairly huge—the inclusion of global communication, ways of making students more aware of audience and purpose, increased attention to visual communication and the representation of data, development of several new assignments, addition of key focus areas in the capstone project that are about engineering practice as well as communication. It's difficult, really, to neatly separate out the effects of the assessments from the larger scope of programmatic development because the assessment data is one piece of how I plan the program, but it always operates in conjunction with all my reading of current literature about both engineering and communication in the disciplines [CID]/communication across the curriculum, rhetoric, student learning theories, assessment, and a range of other things. And that's possible because I have an exceptionally high degree of control and freedom in the CID programs I direct; as long as the students learn to communicate effectively and we pass ABET, I'm left alone to teach and administrate as I see fit.

Professor Jones has done less formal alliance building than Bean did, but her situation was very different. As an untenured professor, she may have been less willing to take on a more high profile role. Also, as she explains, she didn't have a need to garner support because she didn't face much if any resistance to her plans. The College of Engineering was already familiar with the assessment demands of ABET, and she was charged with administering the assessment to satisfy the ABET demands. It seems that the upper administration respected her disciplinary expertise so that she was given the freedom to design an appropriate assessment. She had, as she acknowledged, informal alliances with colleagues in English and across the university through the former WI program. These colleagues, while not playing any formal role, had provided her with support and guidance. Like Bean, she has also used her work in assessment as a basis of scholarship, presenting at conferences and publishing in conference proceedings.

ASSESSING THE WRITING CENTER

Writing centers, like WAC-related programs, serve students beyond one specific department. However, they do not typically operate within the course structure. Instead, they generally work with students from across the campus, one-to-one and/or in workshops, on developing as writers and in completing written work. Writing centers are sometimes affiliated with writing faculty (and/or English departments), but provide support for the entire institution's student population. In some cases, they are positioned as a support service, not an instructional unit, therefore operating outside the department-college structure. Sometimes writing centers are administered by a tenure or tenure-track faculty member and sometimes by an adjunct faculty or a staff member. In short, there are a variety of institutional configurations surrounding these centers and their situation within the institution that need to be considered in designing and implementing a writing center assessment. In the case study we offer below, we see the writing center director meeting the assessment demands of the administration but also expressing a desire to do more substantive assessment based on her disciplinary knowledge.

The writing center at Midwestern University, a comprehensive public institution, operates on the main campus as well as on satellite campuses and serves students across the disciplines. Besides one-to-one tutorials with individual writers, the writing center also works with small groups of students in first-year writing classrooms as well as some other courses. The center is staffed primarily by undergraduate tutors and a few graduate students. The director, a tenured professor whom we call Professor Sadler, is responsible for ongoing assessment. As a rhetoric and composition specialist, Professor Sadler has expertise in writing assessment as well as writing centers.

As part of regular ongoing assessment, Professor Sadler submits an assessment report to the University Assessment Committee and dean every three years. Its most recent report was due in May of 2008. Speaking of assessment generally at Midwestern University, Professor Sadler says that "the university is pretty good" about not discussing writing assessment as "assessment of skills" although she admits "they slip into that discourse, but when you unpack what they mean, they really are more interested in a rhetorically nuanced understanding of writing, rather than a skills-based understanding of writing." She explains that although faculty from across the campus might initially use terms such as "grammar" in reference to student writing, it is apparent in the conversations that the faculty are most interested in issues such as audience and disciplinary conventions for argument that are distinct from grammar and mechanics.

In keeping with this approach to writing, Professor Sadler says writing assessment is generally understood as "necessarily localized." The General Education Committee, of which Professor Sadler was a member, accepted the critiques of standardized tests of writing several years ago. According to Professor Sadler, the assessment people at the university—administrators in the provost's office and in the Faculty Teaching and Learning Center—"get what our department means by localized, collaborative, meaningful assessment." She notes that several of her department's innovative approaches to assessment were highlighted by their regional accreditor as exemplars.

In explaining how writing and assessment is viewed on her campus, Professor Sadler points to the way it is portrayed in the most recent accrediting report:

The writing program is one of the largest programs in the university and is an example of academic rigor institution-wide. In both years of the National Survey of Student Engagement (NSSE), students report having to write multiple drafts more often than their national peers do. Papers tend to be in the middle range for length (five to nineteen pages), a range that allows for multiple drafts.

The evidence of strong writing skills among [the university's] lower division students is attributed to the university's outstanding first-year writing program. Even before prospective freshmen arrive at orientation, information regarding the writing program has been mailed to them so that they can decide in which writing level to enroll.

Students' assessment of their own writing skills at the beginning of their college career is complemented by the assessment of student writing skills at the end of the required first-year course. . . . Students receive instruction, revise and edit papers in a workshop setting, work with writing center consultants within and outside the classroom, and submit a final portfolio of their best work at the end of the term. Students are required to do several revisions of each paper to be included in their final portfolio.

All student writing at the end of the semester is read by two or three faculty who have spent one hour per week norming student outcomes and making those writing expectations transparent to the students in their classes. Assessment is directly integrated with instruction, reinforcing that student grades are meaningful in the public context of the university.

More recently, Professor Sadler and a colleague were able to discuss with the vice provost for Assessment and Accreditation, as well as the director of Institutional Research, the possibility of the university's participation in the Consortium for the Study of Writing in College by including a set of writing-related questions developed by composition professionals (itself an intriguing example of bottom-up assessment) for the NSSE the next time their students are surveyed. The questions added by the Consortium to the NSSE not only include references to the writing center but also to activities the center supports—such as invention, peer review, and revision. Professor Sadler explains that administrators "are receptive to [the NSSE] and see the value of those kinds of questions that get at the behaviors/experiences of students, not just at their ability to produce timed essays." Professor Sadler realizes that her work in other areas of the university—on faculty senate, on the university's retention/enrollment/persistence committee, on the [accreditation] self-study committee—"has more impact on shaping the university's discourse on writing assessment," which is why she thinks it's imperative that writing program and writing center directors be tenure-line faculty who are active in faculty governance and on university-wide committees.

Given this frame for writing and assessment on her campus, Professor Sadler explains that in assessing the writing center, she "tried to identify traits/characteristics of good writing center pedagogy and 'good writing' more generally that connect to traits included in the NSSE writing subset and to what the first-year writing program values." For example, Professor Sadler notes that activities such as brainstorming, collaboration, and peer support are valued in writing center pedagogy and in their first-year curriculum. Because these are already "respected 'talking points' . . . at our university," connecting what the writing center does "to those things will be well received," reasons Professor Sadler. She also is comparing the writing center to other centers because the "provost is very interested in using comparisons to 'aspirant' and 'benchmark' peers in channeling limited funds into best practices for important programs." Because she has some leeway in identifying peer or benchmark institutions, she feels that this process can help her develop the writing center in ways consistent with disciplinary theory and practice. So, she is "trying to position the writing center as one of those essential programs already doing excellent work that others aspire to do (our fellows program, as an example), while also showing that we are sorely administratively understaffed."

In the current writing center assessment, Professor Sadler reports on the number of students served and the types of activities the writing center performs. Beyond simply reporting the numbers, she includes comparisons of the writing center's work to that done at other institutions:

> Within the writing center itself, we conducted 7,759 consultations in the fall and winter terms of the 2007–2008 academic year. Writing consultants also provided approximately 7,254 hours of support in . . . [first-year and advanced writing] classrooms over the 2007–2008 academic year.
>
> According to the Writing Centers Research Project data collected by the University of Louisville, the average number of consultations per year in the writing centers of institutions like [Midwestern] is 1,661. The . . . writing center conducts 367% more than that average number of consultations. In addition, it is rare for a writing center to provide in-classroom support for writing instruction across the university, and rarer still for a writing center to provide consultants in every section of first-year writing.

This comparison, she explains, is part of what the administration values because it situates what is happening at Midwestern within the larger landscape.

She also includes results from exit surveys students complete after a session or at the end of the semester for students who have center consultants working in their classrooms. For example, exit surveys include questions about the students' experiences with the tutors and the help they received:

- Did your writing consultant seem to understand your concerns about writing?

- Was your writing consultant approachable?

- Do you believe that working with the consultant helped you to improve as a writer?

- Would you recommend to other students that they work with this writing consultant?

- What did you and the consultant work on today? Check all that apply.

While the information provided by Sadler about the center's services and student surveys seems typical for writing center assessment, it does not provide direct evidence about student learning and the contribution the writing center makes to it. Professor Sadler is aware of this shortcoming, explaining that the main challenge in conducting a more thorough writing center assessment that might include direct assessment is time. As she explains, she has a half-time release from teaching for administering the writing center, but in addition to directing the center and teaching, she must maintain her scholarly agenda and provide other institutional service. While the center has a full-time secretary who can do the clerical work, Professor Sadler has over fifty undergraduate and graduate student tutors to hire, train, supervise, and mentor to staff four writing center locations. The center also sends writing consultants into all sections of the developmental writing course and the first-year composition course to facilitate small-group peer response workshops and work with writers in the computer lab setting. Professor Sadler explains that working with the writing courses "requires a lot of additional training/mentoring/liaison time that most writing center directors don't deal with."

Fulfilling these responsibilities makes it difficult for her "to do the qualitative, longitudinal research" she sees as necessary for assessment that ascertains the "impact" the writing center has on student writers. She notes that "it is hard to discern what role the writing center has played in a student's writing success. What is attributable to the writing center versus the teacher, the assignments, other courses or experiences?" As she says,

> I truly need to do some qualitative research and examination of tutorials and student writing to better engage with the discussions of students' writing successes on campus. So far, no one questions that the writing center supports student success, but I myself am feeling an urgent need to be able to articulate HOW we offer that success, beyond simply saying "we offer individualized consultations to writers that begin where writers are" and "students feel satisfied

with our services, and report greater writing confidence after working with writing consultants." Those are all important things to say, but I need to explain HOW this all happens in our writing center, and how each service we offer—online, in-classroom, drop-ins, standing appointments—each do that kind of work in different (or similar) ways.

Professor Sadler admits she has "stopped trying to answer this question and instead wants to be able to describe more accurately and fully what working with a writing consultant contributes to a student's writing experience." She is also interested in investigating how working in the writing center contributes to the tutor's learning and development. Despite Professor Sadler's frustration at not being able to conduct "meat-and-potatoes assessment of the impact of the writing center on students' writing or on themselves as writers," she has begun to address these issues in the most recent assessment report "through student self-reporting." But she conveys a sense of frustration at not being able to conduct more through inquiry into the writing center.

Clearly, Professor Sadler understands the complexity of trying to do more than meet the merely bureaucratic demand for an annual assessment report. In our interview, she was quick to point out that the reports don't include all the assessment information she collects, but rather they must be limited to key issues and evidence to address them. The writing center collects many types of less formal information, such as surveys or feedback forms after workshops, that are useful in planning but are not necessarily part of the formal assessment reports she submits.

But despite the challenges she identifies, Professor Sadler finds both the more systematic, formal evaluation and more informal day-to-day assessments very useful in her outreach to both faculty and students on her campus. She explains that the writing center uses information gathered for the assessments in public relations materials—such as flyers about the writing center services, letters to faculty, and other campus-specific materials—as well as in her conversations with faculty and administrators. In fact, she notes that she has even drawn on "writing center assessment facts" in committee and academic senate debates. In all of these situations, she has found that her arguments are more persuasive because she can back up assertions with the information gathered through the assessment process.

CONCLUSION

While each of the case studies offers different insights into how to reframe writing assessment, they also share important characteristics that have contributed to the success of the assessment (and its designers and participants) at both the institutional level and the local program level. (Several, in fact, have also been recognized at a disciplinary level as acknowledged through publications and conference presentations.) The program administrators and faculty members whose work is discussed here use their disciplinary knowledge not only to frame writing assessments consistent with composition theory and practice but also to satisfy the institutional demands they face. In other words, they see and frame the assessments as more than administrative tasks, but as opportunities to build alliances with others and to communicate messages about writing instruction based in their own values as well as values articulated in the field of composition and rhetoric. In doing so, they consider both the challenges and opportunities they face in their local contexts and act accordingly. Sometimes, as at Seaside Community College and Seattle University, the faculty members embrace the assessment as an opportunity to revitalize writing courses in a department and/or across an institution; other times, as at Grand State University, the program administrators focus on smaller, incremental changes as a result of the assessment. However, all of the faculty members leading the assessments consider it as part of the larger framework for the writing program. That is, they have approached it with a sense of what it could do for the program, working across years to implement or change or improve the assessment. They have framed writing assessment as ongoing, evolving, responsive to changes in the programs. Yet, at the same time, they also realize that the assessment and its results change the program. As Professor Bailey at Grand State explains, the portfolio assessment helped to change the program's outcomes, which in turn changed the assessment criteria. Regardless of the program or institution, the writing assessment administrators built alliances—and are still building them—that helped them design, implement, and/or advance the assessment. Sometimes this work was deliberate and directly related to the assessment, as at Seattle, Seaside, and Grand State, while at other times it has been more informal, as at Midwestern and State Tech. In any case, all of these writing professionals understand that effective writing assessment requires collaboration with others whether through formal partnerships or through less formal interactions, such as committee work and conversations with administrators and other campus constituencies.

Finally, at each of these institutions, the writing assessment directors realized that communicating about the assessment—as it is being developed, while it is underway, and afterward—is critical for reframing writing assessment to improve teaching and learning. Assessment, after all, is a powerful form of communication. It tells a story about writing, writers and the teaching of writing. If we want to communicate accurately and effectively about the various components of our programs, we need to consider how we frame the assessment program and how we talk to others about the assessment and its results. As noted on the Council of Writing Program Administrators Assessment Gallery,

> Designing and implementing good assessments is just one part of the work, however.
>
> Another involves helping stakeholders—whether colleagues in the program or department, campus administrators, community members, parents, or legislators—understand what it means to engage in *valid, reliable, and discipline-appropriate assessment that is used to improve teaching and learning.* (Emphasis in original.)

6

REFRAMING ASSESSMENT
Why Does My Participation Matter?

*If we ignore this change and don't try to have a voice to
stem the tide, we're sort of responsible for it happening in a
way. . . . If you're going to be a professional, you have to
look at the larger world that your own system sits within and
think about the relationships between the different levels of
this system. . . . If we don't get involved and try to make the
system better, I think we're abdicating our responsibilities as
professionals.*

Professor Chaco, interview

In the last chapter, we saw how writing instructors and program
administrators in different types of institutions and programs
have used a variety of strategies to reframe writing assessment
on their campuses. We also demonstrated how the efforts of
these writing professionals reflect a number of the strategies
described in chapter four that we believe are essential for this
work: building alliances, thinking about values and actions, and
communicating with stakeholders in a variety of different ways.
In this chapter, we delve more deeply into some of the messy
complexities of reframing writing assessment. We begin by sum-
marizing interviews with two professors who are involved with
this work at the national level, Professors Chaco and Embler.
Both have taught a variety of writing, reading, and English
Language Arts classes and have served in a number of positions within their postsecondary institutions. They also both
have extensive experience working with a variety of nationally
prominent groups who have attempted to effect and continue
to effect educational policy, both at the K–12 and postsecondary level. We then return to the pressing issues facing writing

professionals and present suggestions for how we can work from the strategies described here to reframe writing assessment at the local level and beyond. As important as reframing is for writing professionals, students, and others on local campuses, it is also important because it speaks to issues regarding the assessment of writing (and education more generally) that make up the broader frame surrounding this work.

ACCOUNTABILITY AND EDUCATION

Ready to Assemble: Grading State Higher Education Accountability Systems is a report published by Education Sector, an education policy institute, in 2009 (Adelman and Carey). It is one of many reports published regularly by dozens of think tanks that are working on questions related to education (K–12 and/or postsecondary). The connections between many of these think tanks form a tangled, constantly shifting, web. In a 2008 post, for instance, the blogger Eduwonkette (Jennifer Jennings, now an assistant professor of sociology at Columbia University) outlined connections between "16 big-ticket education policy think tanks and advocacy organizations" including Achieve, Education Trust, the Fordham Institute and the Alliance for Excellence in Education—all names repeated fairly regularly in discussions about education's current challenges and all of whom have proposed various solutions to these problems (2008). In March 2010, Education Sector and the American Enterprise Institute jointly released a report, firmly linking Education Sector to the others included in this web.

Ready to Assemble opens with a story repeated by others who form its interconnected parts about a "tumultuous, highly competitive 21st century economy" where "citizens and workers need knowledge, skills, and credentials in order to prosper"; about how "colleges and universities are falling short" (Adelman and Carey 2009, 1). The report calls, among other things, for "smart, effective higher education accountability systems" (1) that "measure the 'value added' of . . . general education curricul[a] . . . [with] results [that are] comparable across institutions" (2); indicate the time it takes for students to progress toward and earn degrees (3); and look at the extent to which college educations prepare students for careers (3). This opening section, then, seems to repeat stories that fall within the frame dominating discussions about assessment. That story, as we have noted, essentially says that the purpose of education in the twenty-first century is to prepare students in the most efficient ways possible to participate in the global economy (see Apple 1979 for an early discussion of the migration of business metaphors to education). The requirements for this preparation are outlined by those guiding the economy, typically business and professional leaders. But although these ends are clearly defined, the narrative in this frame is that educational systems writ large are "failing"—students are coming to college "underprepared" and thus require "costly remediation," workers are not demonstrating the skills required for success upon hire, and the United States is falling behind as a result.

The outlines of this story, and a frequently invoked solution to the problems identified in it, are readily visible in an anecdote from Craig R. Barrett, chairman of the board at Intel Corporation. The anecdote is included in a chapter of a State Higher Education Executive Officers publication called *More Student Success: A Systemic Solution*; the chapter was jointly authored by Sharmila Basu Conger, a policy analyst from the State Higher Education Executive Officers (SHEEO), and Christine Tell, senior associate for alignment with Achieve. In an address to a meeting of higher education organizations, Barrett

> compared the present position of higher education in the United States to the decline suffered by the semiconductor industry in the 1970s. Functioning as highly autonomous entities, these industry heads shared no "common standards, specifications, or understandings" for input resources. However, by working collaboratively with each other and their suppliers, these leaders were able to create standards across their industry, which helped the industry recover

and surpass its market share. The corollary to postsecondary education was clear: ignoring postsecondary's role in establishing quality
assurance measures for their "input resource" (graduating high
school seniors) puts their own "end product" (postsecondary student success) in jeopardy. (Conger and Tell 2007, 40)

As Conger and Tell repeat it, Barrett's story captures important
elements of this dominant frame. Define the outputs or ends
(semiconductors that can be used across machines, students
who are prepared for particular roles), standardize the inputs
(manufacturing techniques, classes and curricula), and the
product (semiconductors, students who are prepared for the
workforce) will be consistently manufactured. This is one current manifestation of an approach that says assessment should
efficiently identify what's not going right in schools or classes
so those problems can be rapidly solved. It is also one important part of the concept of "accountability," the word most frequently associated with discussions of assessment in this paradigm. Typical of this approach to assessment is a statement in a
document published for legislators by Achieve which says that
"[a]t the core of a good accountability system is information—
the right information provided to the right people at the right
time. As states rethink their . . . accountability systems, they
should start by determining what information is most important
for the people whose efforts are necessary to improve student
readiness" (Conger and Tell 2007, 3).

But the Education Sector report *Ready to Assemble* also
includes language that might be seen as associated with another
perspective on learning, as well. It says,

> In general, researchers agree that students learn more when they're
> actively engaged with their subject matter, professors, and fellow
> students. Students need to be challenged by high expectations and
> given opportunities to solve problems, perform original analysis,
> and get regular, high-quality feedback on their progress. (Adelman
> and Carey 2009, 3)

Terms like *engagement* and *feedback* are sometimes associated with alternatives to the efficiency-driven way of thinking about students. They invoke classrooms, relationships between teachers, students, and learning. They might even be associated with another story about education, one that has made its way around the internet and is repeated by opponents of the technocratic paradigm like historian of education Larry Cuban (2004) and educational activist Susan Ohanian (n.d.).

This story is illustrated in an anecdote from Jamie Vollmer, "a former business executive and attorney [who] now works as a motivational speaker and consultant to increase community support for public schools." When he was an executive at a company whose blueberry ice cream had recently been chosen as "The Best Ice Cream in America," Vollmer spoke at a teacher inservice meeting. At the time, he said, he was

> convinced of two things. . . . [that] public schools needed to change; they were archaic selecting and sorting mechanisms designed for the industrial age and out of step with the needs of our emerging knowledge society . . . [and that] educators were a major part of the problem: they resisted change, hunkered down in their feathered nests, protected by tenure and shielded by a bureaucratic monopoly. They needed to look to business. We knew how to produce quality. Zero defects! TQM! Continuous improvement!

But Vollmer was stopped short by a question from a teacher in the audience. After asking him about the quality of his company's product, she asked what happened when they received a shipment of blueberries that didn't meet their standards. What, then, did they do? In Vollmer's story, this is the moment of epiphany. "In the silence of that room," he says in the version of the story on his Web site,

> I could hear the trap snap . . . I was dead meat, but I wasn't going to lie.
>
> "I send them back."
>
> "That's right!" [the querying teacher] barked, "and we can never send back our blueberries. We take them big, small, rich, poor,

gifted, exceptional, abused, frightened, confident, homeless, rude, and brilliant. We take them with ADHD, junior rheumatoid arthritis, and English as their second language. We take them all! Every one! And that, Mr. Vollmer, is why it's not a business. It's school!" (n.p.)

Vollmer points to this moment as the beginning of his "long transformation" toward the understanding that education is not a process of inputs and outputs, as it is represented by the Intel chief's anecdote in Conger and Tell (2007). That is, it is not possible to set benchmarks and assume they can be uniformly achieved if all subjects working toward those benchmarks are administered the same treatment (e.g., if they all are subjects to and of the same instructional practices). Instead, schools must deal with each student as she or he comes, individually. Teachers must recognize and build upon what students know, and share stories of their successes.

THE MESSY REALITIES OF COMPROMISE

Ready to Assemble and the anecdotes from Conger and Tell and Vollmer seem to capture two different perspectives on education and schooling. But they don't illustrate the kind of complicated and messy wrestling associated with assessment work at the local level described by the program directors and instructors in the previous chapter, nor the kind of navigation in which Professor Embler and Professor Chaco have participated at the local and national levels. To think about these more complicated issues of compromise and negotiation, then, we summarize stories both of them tell about their day-to-day experiences working with organizations, individuals, and policy institutes attempting to shape education policy.

Professor Chaco: The Fine Line Between Compromise and "Going to the Mat"

Professor Chaco has worked with several efforts that have convened individuals from a variety of arenas—K–12 teachers, employers, members of the armed forces, K–12 and

postsecondary administrators, state school professionals—
under the auspices of education reform linked to policy initiatives in her home state, as well as at the national level. She
is a content expert on writing as well as reading and English
Language Arts, and she brings long perspective as a teacher and
teacher educator to this work. In her experience, those around
the table for these discussions

> bring different ideas about what writing is and what students should
> learn, and they're legitimate—legitimately different. Because they
> come, say, from different disciplines or career paths where differ-
> ent kinds of writing are privileged more than others, or used more
> than others in certain communities . . ., [they] have different ideas
> about what students need to be able to know . . . to be successful in
> the world of work or college. The ideas center around definitions
> of writing. A lot of the debates . . . [are] around how [to] articulate
> what's important.

Based on this experience, Professor Chaco asks what we see
as a crucial question for those involved with reframing writing
through assessment: "How do you articulate what's important,
and how do you incorporate all of these perspectives in a way
that doesn't do real damage to one group [of the participants in
these discussions]?" These participants all come with different
"driving forces"—what we call, in chapter four, interests—that
motivate their positions. Some are thinking about the workforce, while others are thinking more in terms of "being well-
educated citizens." At the same time, though, they *are* all thinking about what is necessary for students to be successful—but
they have different ideas about what success means, and how
to achieve it.

Ultimately, these different ideas about success spin out into
different ideas about the educational policies that will shape
what students learn. And here, says Professor Chaco, is where
the on-the-ground realities of policy work become even more
complicated. "Sometimes, you have groups of people with
really different backgrounds with varying degrees of experience

with schools, and [some of them] come up with unrealistic ideas . . . that might actually in the end do harm to schools. Not intentionally at all, but they're ideas that [these people] think for one reason or another are important."

In her experience, Professor Chaco has had moments when the various participants in these discussions and efforts have "[found] commonalities and middle ground." To illustrate, she uses a hypothetical example about the idea of "research."

> One of the things important to teachers, is, say, students doing extended projects that involve working with sources and using research. They're concerned with things like evaluating the credibility of the research. But let's say there's another professional there at the table where the work that writing does in the profession is reporting on what happened. So there may be a focus on different genres [and] the task is to find a way to allow both of these to coexist [by saying, perhaps, that] "there's a variety of different genres that might be used in different ways in different professions."

We would call the attention to a focus on genres an instance of successful issue-based alliance building. In listening to other participants, Professor Chaco says, it can be possible to discern their interests and construct policy and assessment that may bridge seeming divergences. Another strategy Professor Chaco has used with success in these discussions is drawing on her extensive experience as a teacher and a teacher of teachers to paint a sort of verbal portrait about the everyday realities of schools. "It's kind of like saying, 'Here, look at my world,'" she says. Without this information, though, attempts to identify shared interests and develop compromise positions can quickly falter. "A lot of times, [participants in these discussions, *including* college writing teachers] are just really unaware of conditions in K–12 schools. So when you have discussions about what should be done, sometimes there are unrealistic expectations. . . . Because of a myriad of things—scheduling, money, the traditional way that things get done in a particular community, lots of reasons—there is also a lack of awareness about what the other community's constraints . . . and perspectives are, and that breaks down the conversation that can lead to finding commonality."

But while these anecdotes are helpful, Professor Chaco says, they are not enough—engaging in and sharing results of rigorous, systematic research is also an essential strategy for participating in these larger discussions. "I've turned to research, thinking that we can learn from failed experiments [as well]. Because when you make decisions, you want to be vigilant about monitoring what the impact is. Hypothetically, if you have a single sample assessment or a multiple-choice assessment or a portfolio assessment, what happens? What are the implications? A lot of the time in education reform, people don't take the time" to engage in the research to think about these questions.

Professor Chaco also points to approaches or attitudes that can prevent this kind of compromise work, as well. Sometimes, she has tried "persuasion, educating people about what schools are like" but "people just refused to see it from the other person's perspective." Sometimes—in what we might think of as the best outcome—"people stop listening to those people." But other times, she says, these discussions can go too far. "[People] can't [come] into these discussions with something that's wrongheaded, or so prescriptive," she says. They don't think, or don't realize, how their efforts affect curriculum and student experience. "It's a huge task, and you can't do it overnight." Sometimes, she says, "there have been times where I've just gone to the mat and said, 'It's not feasible.'" She says she knows when she needs to take this stance based on "a lot of years of experience working with schools and having had experiments that didn't work." And one of the problems she's encountered in recent policy work is that there are a number of participants in these discussions who "haven't had experience in schools or lived in that world," so they aren't familiar with these everyday realities. At the same time, "decisions [are being made] with little regard to the impact that they will have."

Another challenge Professor Chaco observes is that it is becoming increasingly clear that there are strongly competing visions of education operating in policy discussions today. She references Linda Darling-Hammond's work (e.g., 2004) to describe "two worlds." In one, she says, "teachers are viewed as professionals who take responsibility for their work, who talk across borders, try to create links, articulate curriculum, research their practice . . . and in this other world, it's more top-down research and development where someone else gives results to teachers and tells them what to do with it." The problem, though, is that "in the last ten to fifteen years things have gone downhill in a frightening way because of the increasing reliance on assessments that are poorly conceived, and people don't research, or don't pay attention to research, on the negative impact [they are having in] schools." But we all have a responsibility, she says, to get involved—as her epigraph to this chapter says, "If we don't, . . . we're abrogating our responsibilities as professionals."

Professor Embler: "Planting Seeds" and the "Honorable Compromise"

Professor Embler also believes writing instructors and program directors have a responsibility to get involved in discussions about assessment, its terms, and the practices associated with those terms. An English professor and former writing program director, Professor Embler has worked extensively for national organizations, both those that are discipline specific and those that encompass education more broadly. She has a wide range of experiences working directly with policymakers and legislators to help shape education policies, specifically those related to assessment and literacy, at both the K–12 and higher education levels. Like Professor Chaco, she draws on her knowledge and experience as an educator and researcher in this work, "applying what we know about writing and writing assessment" in discussions about education held in the wider community.

Like Professor Chaco, Professor Embler has seen that, in discussions about education and policy, different groups (e.g., teachers and those working with or for educational policy organizations) hold beliefs and assumptions that are often at odds one another. For example, in reference to talk about assessment and higher education, she notes that different groups involved in discussions (or debates) about assessment are both missing the opportunities of assessment, and are at odds with one another over the ways assessment is described. "Many academics," she says, "are not acculturated to the potential of assessment for student learning." At the same time, for many policymakers and public audiences, "testing equals assessment." And while many teachers bristle at this equation, they aren't able to come up with positive alternatives to reframe the discussion. These differences come from dissimilar "frames for learning" held by the parties involved in these discussions, according to Professor Embler. "In most education circles, all tend to share the belief that students can learn and that learning is complex and multifaceted. But, as it bubbles up in policy discussions, there is limited understanding of learning and what it means to learn." Her role, in these kinds of discussions, is often to help the other parties—whether academics or policymakers—understand what research says about assessment and learning in relationship to the issues on the table.

The "lessons learned" from her work with different groups apply across varied contexts but are especially pertinent when working on public policy. "Collaboration is key," she explains. Like Professor Chaco, she says that "give and take is critical in the policy realm." This kind of work means that all parties "have to be willing to listen and learn" from each other. One can't enter the discussion too entrenched in one's position or collaboration can't happen. By maintaining the focus on the "big picture" and "long term goals," Professor Embler explains, one can come to "an honorable compromise." This kind compromise can help us make "incremental change" so we can get closer to our goals. "The power of the status quo makes any change difficult. Even if something is not effective, it is already in place [so] change is hard for people. If we withdraw, get angry, or don't even enter these more public discussions, then we aren't able to have any influence at all, and it is unlikely that our values and perspectives will be represented."

The second important lesson, according to Professor Embler, is to "take the initiative." It's important, she advises, to act. For example, she explains that when she was a writing program administrator, she had heard talk about placement mandates that would apply to all state institutions coming down from the state level. Instead of waiting until something was imposed on them, she initiated a state-wide meeting of writing program directors to deal with the concerns. This kind of action, which also included collaborating with others who would be affected by state policy, provided them with the opportunity to address the concerns and educate appropriate constituencies about placement before a policy was developed and implemented.

Other kinds of initiatives may be less focused on a particular issue but can help by "planting seeds" so that when a particular issue does become the focus of public policy debates, there is already more awareness about it. For example, she offers an idea she championed many years ago: each writing program director or department chair should speak to one community group a year about writing and the teaching of writing. In this way, we would already be engaging with the public about important issues and educating them about what research tells us about teaching writing and learning to write so that later, when an issue related to writing is being debated, we can "harvest" what we planted. This type of action, she continues, can allow us "to frame the questions" and show how research can help provide answers. "If we are all doing this, there is the potential to change the discussion about teaching and learning and assessment over time."

Writing program faculty and directors, she contends, are better positioned to do this kind of work than many other academics because typically they are already experienced at working outside their own disciplines and departments. With assessment issues, Professor Embler believes it is especially important to be proactive because "assessment is profoundly influential in student learning." She acknowledges that in higher education, faculty members and institutions have been slow to provide scalable alternatives to assessments developed by testing companies. "Because money has been channeled into testing companies, much assessment evidence used in state and federal policy making comes through these companies," she contends. "Because these tests are run on a large scale and have longitudinal results available, their use is powerful and hard to change." Just as K–12 educators are speaking up to influence assessments being developed for standards used across states, higher education faculty need to be informed about and to influence large-scale assessments of learning in higher education. In fact, it is "critical" that we "work across K–12 and college around assessment, while respecting each other's experiences and expertise."

In terms of working specifically with policymakers, Professor Embler notes that "the culture around . . . politics and how to influence policy is different than in other venues." She explains that "being in the right place at the right time and being prepared" is critical. For example, education is just one of many important issues that legislators and their staffers have to deal with. So, if she gets a call from an aide, she needs to be ready to provide the necessary information quickly and in accessible language. She tries to think about it as "how can I help them understand X?" Timing is also critical, so if she isn't prepared when asked for information, then she misses an opportunity, and she may not get another chance to influence the discussion of that issue. Of course, she admits, one also needs to try to "create opportunities."

Professor Embler's "lessons learned" echo those used by community organizers and presented in chapter four. Like Alinsky, she feels it is important to build alliances and take action. Her recommendations fall into what we call issue-based alliance building, an approach that draws from both interest- and values-based work. In other words, a short-term interest might be the impetus to bring a group together; by understanding each others' values and goals, a more long-term relationship can be formed. Of course, as Professor Embler explains, sometimes the other parties involved aren't willing to collaborate and don't come to the discussion in good faith. When that happens, she says, she opts out if possible. Experience has helped her become better at determining if the other parties are acting in good faith. However, she also admits that sometimes in public policy circles, she doesn't always have the option of not working with the other parties.

In today's climate, Professor Embler feels there is "more of a sense of urgency about ways we educate and outcomes of it for college and workplace readiness and there is a new emphasis on being competitive in the global economy." This urgency, she says, means that there is a push to make change happen "instead of letting [ideas] percolate through all constituencies." She mentioned the Common Core State Standards Initiative as "an example of moving so quickly there was insufficient time for percolation through all affected constituencies, especially teachers. The result is less consonance and agreement about the final product than might have been possible."

Given the current climate, Professor Embler believes (much like Professor Chaco) that we as academics are obligated to participate in these public debates. "We all have the responsibility to participate and use our knowledge to move the discussion [about education] forward." She identifies several ways academics can influence policy discussions while also recognizing the obstacles that need to be overcome. Researchers "should always be thinking about public audiences, not just academic ones, for their results." She explains that we "need to feed scholarly results into the system." This means we must use our rhetorical knowledge to adapt what we have to contribute so that it is appropriate for nonacademic audiences. We also need to value the work that extends beyond the academy, whether it is writing for public audiences, engaging in public debates on issues related to our expertise, or serving on local or national commissions to address issues. Too often this work, she explains, is not considered intellectual work and so is dismissed as service. However, Professor Embler argues that we in the academy can change this situation by working through the faculty governance structure and by serving in leadership positions. We can start, she says, by getting involved in these activities on our own campuses. Writing program faculty and administrators, she emphasizes, are already "poised and prepared" for this work on their campuses and in the wider community.

BOUNDARIES AND UNITS OF ANALYSIS: THE DILEMMA OF REFRAMING [WRITING] ASSESSMENT

The anecdotes from Barrett and Vollmer represent efforts to grapple with a set of issues that have occupied center stage in discussions about colleges and universities since the nineteenth century, and the work in which Professors Chaco and Embler are engaged represents efforts to address these issues both tactically and strategically. Broadly, they address questions around what constitutes higher education: What is this system, and what are its purposes? Where do its boundaries lie? How is it possible, within those boundaries, to learn about what is happening within it? How can it be improved? At the level of the institution, these questions also persist: What is a university? Where does it stop and start? What does it do, how, and why?

The work of nineteenth-century educators like Charles Eliot (discussed in chapter three) represents one attempt to recreate the boundaries of the academy, moving them away from an effort to cultivate the aesthetic sensibilities of a cultural elite and toward a focus on preparation of members of that elite for careers associated with the nation's burgeoning industrial development. This focus also facilitated a shift in the boundaries around the educational meritocracy, associating it more firmly with economic achievement and repurposing education to focus on the production of knowledge and workers. At the same time, members of the academy—professors and instructors—shifted the basis of their professional authority toward knowledge and practices based in their disciplines, rather than in local communities. The result, in part, was to distinguish professional expertise in one discipline from that in another and to reinforce the conception of "the university" as something analogous to a loosely aligned set of nation states. Within this conception of the academy, each discipline was to provide its students with the content knowledge and professional behaviors determined by its members to be associated with academic training in that discipline (Bender 1993). This was often to be done in consultation with external professionals—especially in applied fields like science and engineering—but academic professionals were still invested with the authority to prepare students through educational training (Noble 1985).

Another outcome of this work, emphasized by Professor Chaco in her discussion (and reified by the differences in secondary and postsecondary accreditation described in part in chapter two), was a split between secondary and postsecondary education that created, in essence, two relatively distinct systems. "A lot of the time," Professor Chaco says, "college writing teachers are just unaware of conditions in K–12 schools. . . . The lack of communication between the two [groups of teachers] means that there's this group of students coming up being prepared in ways that college teachers find problematic when [students] get there, but then [some] college teachers fill up the moat and pull up the drawbridge and don't bother themselves with what's happening in K–12." This difference also stems, in part, from the movement toward academic disciplines, which also reified distinct differences between "content" experts and "pedagogy." As Professor Embler expresses it, academics are enculturated into a discipline, and their sense of self is "based in the discipline."

With the social and economic upheaval of the mid- to late twentieth century, academic disciplines found their essentially isolationist stance threatened by the same forces that led to the construction of their boundaries during the 1890s, 1900s, and 1910s. That is, as the voices and values associated with Civil Rights and other midcentury movements found purchase within the broader culture, and as more non-white, non-middle class students were admitted to colleges and universities, members of the academy found themselves encountering new ideologies and values within their classrooms as well as outside of them. One prominent response, as Richard Ohmann (2000) has noted, was for higher education to latch on to concepts from industry, such as the notion of "accountability" and the import of business-associated practices like Total Quality Management (TQM), in an attempt to quickly assert control over both the boundaries surrounding "the academy" from the outside and the content that filled those boundaries, like curriculum and the practices of academic workers, from the inside.

In early twenty-first-century discussions of assessment and "accountability" like those described in chapters one, two, and above, these issues of demarking territories within the academy once again have emerged front and center. In part because the business-oriented approach cited by Ohmann (2000) has become so dominant, the focus on assessment is a seemingly natural extension of this movement that began in the late nineteenth and early twentieth centuries. Stemming from the issues circulating in that movement, the questions about purposes and audiences for assessment discussed in chapter two and raised in Professor Chaco's example are omnipresent. What should constitute the unit of analysis in an assessment? Should it be the student? A classroom? A program? A college or university? How should the boundaries around these units of analysis be drawn, and by whom? What should be the purpose(s) of the assessment? For instance, if students are the unit of analysis, should it be to prove that they are learning what they should, or that their teachers are teaching the things the students should learn in the best ways? If an institution is the unit of analysis, should the purpose of the assessment be to show that the institution is achieving some goal(s) in a prescribed period? Alternatively, should it be to engage individuals and groups involved in learning (whether inside or outside the academy) in a dialogue about what is being learned, why, and how that might be described and developed?

In arenas outside of academe, discussions about assessment and/or the purpose and function of education (at all levels) tend to focus on determining or demonstrating institutional effectiveness for audiences outside the academy. These efforts typically involve outlining the broadest possible boundaries—a K–12 system of education, an entire college or university, even a cluster of institutions seen as "comparable" in some way—and then using large-scale assessments to determine whether the institution is effectively achieving outcomes determined (often by the creators of the assessments, who typically have advisory boards or other processes for input) to be important for all students within the defined boundaries. This approach is evident, for instance, in "Improving Student Learning in Higher Education through Better Accountability and Assessment," a discussion paper published by the National Association of State Universities and Land Grant Colleges (now Association of Public and Land Grant Universities) that was a precursor to the Voluntary System of Accountability. "More than 40 states have created some form of accountability or statistical reporting system and more than half of those have formal report cards that characterize learning outcomes, including more than 200 performance indicators that were directly or indirectly tied to student learning," the document says. But "the current accountability structures suffer from several flaws—the systems are often fragmented . . . and the data themselves are not always effectively communicated or understood by stakeholders." (McPherson and Shulenberger 2006, n.p.)

Thus, among other things, this document suggests that

[a]n approach that combines measures of educational effectiveness with measures of a few key competencies, done with statically adequate samples, may be able to provide some understanding of how individual colleges and universities compare within their type of institutions and also help the institutions improve their learning process.

and

> [a] successful voluntary system would need to trust in the validity of its instruments. Considerations should be given to asking the National Academy of the Sciences to survey the existing learning assessment instruments and explore the gaps and inconsistencies. Some areas of research probably are already clear so evaluative work could be completed on these quickly. As institutions proceed towards a voluntary system, it would be important to begin with trial tests as needed with samples of institutions. (McPherson and Shulenberger 2006, n.p.)

Inside the academy, and especially inside our field of composition and rhetoric, assessment efforts have centered around student learning and development and, sometimes, on organizational (institutional) improvement. Those involved in these efforts have also sometimes raised questions about how the idea of "effective application of learning" often raised in discussions about learning outside the academy can be useful for these more internally focused efforts. At the same time, they have argued strongly that literacy practices are local and contextual, and that evidence of effective learning lies in the ability to adapt and continue to learn, rather than to immediately manifest skills required in specific situations and/or workplaces. The opening paragraph of the NCTE-WPA White Paper on Writing Assessment in Colleges and Universities (which both of us helped to draft), for instance, notes that "[a] preponderance of research argues that literacy and its teaching are socially contextualized and socially constructed dynamics, evolving as people, exigency, context, and other factors change. The varied language competencies and experiences with which students come to the classroom can sometimes conflict with what they are taught or told to value in school. The assessment of writing, therefore, must account for these contextual and social elements of writing pedagogy and literacy" (National Council of Teachers of English/Council of Writing Program Administrators 2008).

This research leads to principles crucial for classroom and program assessment: it should be locally based, locally determined, and used to improve teaching and learning on the local level (Council of Writing Program Administrators Assessment Gallery 2008). The first two principles in the CCCC position statement on writing assessment, principles taken into account in the NCTE-WPA white paper, also make the point that assessments must be locally grounded and used to improve local practice, and that assessments should be designed in response to "local goals, not external pressures" (Conference 2006).

Documents like those produced by CCCC and NCTE-WPA (as well as the case studies we featured in chapter five) attest to the acumen with which composition instructors can, by now, undertake *locally based* assessments that reflect principles and practices recognized as valid both within the educational assessment literature and within the principles outlined by our own discipline. These assessments provide the kind of specific illustrations that Professors Chaco and Embler describe as useful in their work shaping public policy, and also can constitute the kind of assessment research they believe is essential for this work. Chris Anson puts these activities in the context of an "open system," one where "writing is situated in social practice and therefore context-dependent" (2009, 116). That is, we are able to work from a statement used in the opening of the Council of Writing Program Administrators Assessment Gallery, which includes the White Paper and specific models of assessments that reflect the principles outlined in that document: "Valid and reliable assessment is consistent at the level of principle and conceptualization: it is discipline-based, locally determined, and used to inform teaching and learning at the local level." It is repeated in syntheses like O'Neill, Moore, and Huot's *Guide to College Writing Assessment,* which notes that "[i]f we believe that literacy activities or events occur within—and reflect—a social context . . . then assessment (itself a literacy activity or event) must account for context in order to yield meaningful results" (2009, 60). They also outline the consequences of ignoring or eliding the need to ground assessment in local contexts, citing listserv posts or conference presentations in which instructors ask for and/or "promote a particular assessment model or rubric, as if assessment methodology can be readily transported between schools and departments or even between disciplines" (60).

But as important as these efforts are—and we think that they are absolutely crucial—they do not yet effectively speak to the dilemma addressed by David Shupe (2008) and Lynn Priddy (2009) that we discussed in chapter two: the multiple purposes and audiences for assessment and the challenge of addressing some of the concerns raised by those who are not already insiders in postsecondary education, such as the need to demonstrate that students are leaving college equipped to engage in particular kinds of thinking and/or doing. Currently, assessments designed to speak to this concern invoke technocratic, behavioralist definitions to address key terms like "effectiveness." How many students are graduating? If x, y, and z are determined to be important indicators of learning, what percentage of students are achieving x, y, and z at a score that is determined to be evidence of effective manifestation of these skills? How much are students' grades rising or falling as they move through an education? What is their time to degree? How many credits are they being awarded for how many hours in class, and why? While we might think we can ignore these questions and discussions extending from them, we'll return to one of Professor Chaco's statements. College writing professionals, she says, don't often ask what to do about the dilemma of large-scale assessment. "You can just say, 'it's bad'—and yes, there are a lot of bad things about it. But if we don't get involved and try to make the system better, . . . we're abrogating our responsibilities as professionals."

To be sure, there are excellent *critiques* of large-scale assessment practices within our field. Researchers have demonstrated that these exams do not predict what they claim to (e.g., Haswell 2005a); that they privilege features of writing (such as length), reading (such as the depositing of information), and information use (such as encouraging students to misuse information) that undermine practices generally associated with "an educated person" (regardless of whether "education" is linked to critical citizenship or preparation for work) (e.g., Perelman 2009); that the research upon which they are based is self-referential (e.g., Adler-Kassner 2008; Garan 2005; Huot 2007); and that the questions they ask are flat-out inappropriate (e.g, Sommers 2009). These critiques, for the most part, are written by us, for us, and published in venues that reach us. Yet, others—such as policymakers, special interest groups, corporate CEOs—are constructing the frames that surround these questions and define teaching and learning. We can't influence how these frames are shaped and reshaped unless we engage them more directly.

In addition to reframing writing assessment at the local level, then, writing instructors, program directors, and others must also get involved at this larger level so that we can contribute to discussions about the meaning of terms like *effectiveness*, or even *college and career readiness*. We might ask what it means, for example, to be prepared for college or work? What does it mean for an institution to be effective? The problem, though, is that while composition instructors and researchers have research, language, and models upon which to discuss the importance, validity, and/or necessity of locally based assessments, we haven't yet developed the discourse (and concomitant understandings of concepts and practices reflected in and underscoring that discourse) to participate fully in discussions about large-scale assessment currently dominating the educational policy literature and popular discussions about education. Not only do we need to learn how to engage more effectively in these discussions, we also need to value this kind of work, as Professor Embler reminds us.

GETTING TO YES: RECONCEPTUALIZING REFRAMING

Critiques that identify theoretical conflicts are an important first step in contributing to the ongoing discussions about large-scale assessment because they identify fallacies of method, logic, and construction in existing models. And articulating these critiques is important because they situate the assessments and issues associated with them within our own disciplinary expertise. But one of the most important lessons that community organizers, media strategists, and political activists alike took from the mid-1990s is that going beyond just critique is absolutely crucial. In fact, pointing out what is wrong does not provide anyone a handhold for acting upon what is right—in other words, it doesn't provide the foundation for a proactive strategy that can reframe issues important to us. Instead, it puts us only in a reactive mode—and reaction, in the long run, only perpetuates the issues being critiqued in the first instance. This was the case, for instance, when a group of postsecondary writing instructors (including us) wanted to respond to a draft of the Common Core State Standards issued in late 2009. One of the most valuable lessons of George Lakoff's *Don't Think of An Elephant*, a point he makes on the first page, is that "[w]hen we negate a frame, we evoke the frame" (2004, 3; also see Nunberg, 2006). In our case, if we say "Writing can't be measured" to communicate the idea that writing is not quantifiable as a process or product, we are reinforcing the measurement frame.

Instead, we need to state our ideas in ways that don't restate the concept we are attempting to reframe but in language that is accessible. For example, one of the National Writing Project's messages is "Writing is essential to thinking." We also need to find a way to work beyond the local, yet maintain research-based principles emphasizing the local and contextual nature of literacy practices that is the cornerstone of much of our field's research and teaching. And we absolutely need to speak to— and, perhaps more importantly, build alliances with—others *outside* our disciplines and even our institutions to make a difference. This means identifying questions, models, and language that reflect what we want, rather than what we do not want— and making sure questions and models speak to concerns articulated by those outside the academy, those interested parties who Professor Chaco reminds us have a legitimate reason to care about what happens in writing classes.

Three recent efforts—two by a group of composition instructors and one by the Association of American Colleges and Universities that is also part of the grant funding a pilot study as part of the Voluntary System of Accountability—illustrate attempts to confront this challenge and provide lessons from which we might draw.

Inter-institutional Writing Assessment: Comparable Yet Local

The first effort is described by the participants (who co-authored an article in *College Composition and Communication*) as an "inter-institutional" effort to assess writing (Pagano et al. 2008). In this effort, six institutions (later five, after one left the pilot study), funded by a FIPSE grant, designed an assessment study that would creatively approach issues associated with public discussions of what college students learn—including institutional effectiveness, comparability, and demonstration of student learning. (Another earlier example of this kind of inter-institutional collaboration can be seen in the Portnet project, which involved writing teachers from across the country reading and discussing student work from one another's institutions. [For more on Portnet see Allen 1995.]) As five of the study's coordinators explain, this pilot was designed to try to address what is a frequent tension between local assessments (useful within the program or institution) and the call to "determine better ways to assess individual change and establish effectiveness, relative to national norms, or if not in terms of norms, at least with results contextualized beyond the local institution" (Pagano et al. 2008, 287).

In the pilot study, the five institutions decided to focus their assessment around an outcome shared by all the programs, "responding to a text." The authors explain that "reading, engaging with, and responding to a text in the form of a critical or analytic paper is both a common and important academic task" (Pagano et al. 2008, 292). Within this broad concept, however, each institution defined the "text[s]" with which students would work (in some cases these were written, in others they came from observation, in others they were multimedia texts) (293–294).

Through an ambitious collaborative process of reading, rubric development, and rating, study participants ultimately made productive discoveries within their institutions' writing programs: that on the vast majority of measures (with only one small exception), writing instruction did indeed seem to positively affect students' writing performance and thus "add value" (Pagano et al. 2008, 300). Participants also found the process of collaboration, and of study development, valuable for their institutions and programs, a result that is borne out across many other published descriptions of assessment studies (see, for example, Broad et al. 2009; the Council of Writing Administrators Assessment Assessment Gallery; the discussion on portfolios in chapter three; and the case studies we reported in chapter five).

When it came to the issue of inter-institutional comparison, this study also yielded important results that speak to the issue of reframing. First, participants found that "the more selective the institution, the higher the scores" (Pagano et al. 2008, 298). This suggests, certainly, that for the purposes of inter-institutional comparability, "selectivity" is an important factor to consider. Indeed, in the Integrated Postsecondary Education Data System (IPEDS), "selectivity" appears as one of the "frequently used variables" in requests for institution-specific information. (If readers have not had occasion to search IPEDS, we urge you to do so—go to http://nces.ed.gov/IPEDS/ and click on "College Navigator" for this specific function.) More relevant for the purposes of this discussion, though, are the reflections on the localized nature of writing instruction that came from the authors' analysis. "Perhaps the most interesting result from this part of the analysis," they write, "is the dominating influence of the students' institutional contexts" (2008, 303). They continue:

We believe that the proponents of accountability assessment who advocate for "interstate" or "one size fits all" comparisons likely envision the type of comparison afforded by standardized exams. . . . Such [exams] would locate institutions—and students—relative to an anonymous norming population. . . . [W]e found differences between institutions, but we knew who it was who was being compared, and we could make sense of the findings. When it came time to measure progress, we compared our students to themselves, not to national norms or percentile ranks. (Pagano et al. 2008, 303)

In assessing for "value added," then, it is essential to understand "value added" to what? What are the local factors that define where students started at the particular institution? To understand the local, the assessment and the interpretation of its results need to take into consideration the local: the students, the instruction, the curriculum. Attending to these features, the researchers say, "generates assessment data that are sensitive to learning and skill improvement at the individual level, exactly where we want to be assessing gain" (Pagano et al. 303). This conclusion echoes findings long stressed in the field's policy documents and research—in order to locate value in the findings of assessment projects, the criteria used in those projects must be rooted in the specific, local context of the institution and its students. This, in turn, reaffirms one of composition and literacy studies' fundamental tenets: literacy practices and literacy development must be located in the specific, local experiences of those participating in those practices (see, for example, Gee 1996).

In addition to providing evidence for conceptualizations of assessment stemming from existing research, Pagano et al.'s discussion of their study highlights the challenge of addressing questions about "accountability" or demonstrations of learning. When we compare institutions, they say, we must be able to attend to the local contexts of the institutions. That would seem to send us right back to the issues raised earlier, about competing and possibly conflicting responses to questions about the units of analysis for assessment (Students in a writing class? A program? An institution? Three institutions compared to one another?) and how the boundaries around units of analysis should be drawn (By the average SAT scores of students? By time to degree? By retention or persistence data?).

As we read Pagano et al.'s analysis, we see an argument to *reframe* responses to these questions, pushing against the model emanating from the dominant frame that relies primarily on IPEDS data and/or standardized test scores (ACT or SAT for students entering college; increasingly, with the dominance of the Voluntary System of Accountability, scores on standardized exams like the Collegiate Assessment of Academic Progress and Proficiency [CAAP, an ACT product], the Measure of Academic Proficiency and Progress [MAPP, an SAT product], or the Collegiate Learning Assessment [CLA, produced by the Collegiate Education Association]). As Diane Auer Jones, former assistant secretary for postsecondary education in the U.S. Department of Education notes, using these data "is like making policy decisions for the nation based on the profile and performance of a single state" (2009, 35).

Cross-Institutional Assessment: Bottom-Up Development of an Adaptable Rubric for Student Work

A project that has gone even farther to try to address the challenging dilemma of developing locally grounded assessments that speak to external requests for demonstration of learning, and the development of comparable data, is the AAC&U Valid Assessment of Learning in Undergraduate Education (VALUE) project. (In the interest of full disclosure, we should note that Linda was on the team that worked on the Written Communication rubric for this project.) AAC&U's work parallels that of the American Diploma Project (ADP) in the sense that it, too, surveyed employers in highly desirable fields, and also worked with postsecondary faculty to identify important features associated with learning. However, where ADP's guidelines for "college and career readiness" focus on carefully defined skills represented in specific products, AAC&U's more broadly address strategies—habits of mind—represented in practices. (It is worth noting, too, that ADP's work does not extend to developing specific assessments, as the AAC&U VALUE project has.)

The distinction can be seen, for instance, in the differences between the ways something like "inquiry" is defined in a report like *Ready or Not* from ADP, and one like *College Learning for the New Global Century* from AAC&U. *Ready or Not* says research, as a process of inquiry, "requires the ability to frame, analyze, and solve problems, while building on the contributions of others. As future college students or employees, students will be asked to hone these essential skills with increasing sophistication" (Achieve 2004, 29). *Ready or Not* then goes on to lay out distinct expectations, each cross-referenced to a specific college and/or career readiness standard, that reflect this definition, ultimately leading to "an extended research essay (approximately six to ten pages), building on primary and secondary sources, that . . . [m]arshals evidence in support of a clear thesis statement and related claims; [p]araphrases and summarizes with accuracy and fidelity the range of arguments and evidence supporting or refuting the thesis . . . "; and cites sources and other included information accurately (34).

Alternatively, the Association of American Colleges and Universities (AAC&U) *College Learning for the New Global Century*, a report also grounded in employer surveys, frames learning within interrelated, cross-disciplinary learning outcomes. "Inquiry and analysis" is included in key "intellectual and practical skills" that will be required of students (AAC&U 2007, 12); however, the report details repeatedly the ways in which all of the outcomes, including inquiry, "can and should be addressed in different ways across varied fields of study. Engineers," it says, "use quite different inquiry and communication skills than anthropologists. . . . Even effective writing takes different forms in different fields and settings" (2007, 14). "Because competence is always related to context," it continues, "[t]his report does not recommend teaching 'skills' apart from content and context" (2007, 14). Inquiry in this sense, then, is "cross-disciplinary" (2007, 20), and the shape of the questions, processes for investigation, and products that come from research depend in which the inquiry is taking place. Rather than outline the required skills and outcomes, the AAC&U report calls for education to allow students to "engage the big questions" through "inquiry-based learning" where students "learn how to find and evaluate evidence, how to consider and assess competing interpretations, how to form and test their own analyses and interpretations, how to solve problems, and how to communicate persuasively" (2007, 30).

Extending from this focus on broad strategies and practices rather than specific skills, the development of the VALUE rubric for written communication began with a review by writing instructors and program directors of existing assessment processes from courses and programs. Based on this review of existing work, the written communication team then engaged in an eighteen-month process to design a rubric that could be used inside and outside of writing classrooms to evaluate actual course artifacts collected in an electronic portfolio. While the final rubric (which can be found on the VALUE website at http://www.aacu.org/value/) is fairly broad, it reflects three qualities we associate with best practices in assessment. First, it was developed by disciplinary professionals through an examination of local assessment work. Second, it is intended to be used with actual student work produced in the context of a course, and explicitly requests contexts for the materials (e.g., assignment sheets, student reflections) as a part of the collected material. Third, it is prefaced by a statement explaining that the best assessment practices should be locally grounded, recommending that the rubric be seen as a beginning for discussions about assessment rather than the end of one (AAC&U 2009).

As VALUE Director and AAC&U Vice President for the Office of Quality, Curriculum and Assessment Terrel Rhodes notes, this project was conceived as a direct response to the impetus to use what we are here referring to as technocratic assessment measures to shape the boundaries of learning and comparability. Rhodes explains that

> [c]alls for greater accountability for student learning have focused . . . on the simplest of indicators related to student success, e.g. retention and graduation rates. It is important that students who come to higher education remain and successfully complete their studies, of course. However, it is even more important that our students actually learn what we have determined is critical and that they do so at a high level of quality. To date, the emphasis from policy makers and many higher education leaders has been to rely on standardized test scores as proxy measures for quality student learning on our campuses.
>
> Given that most campuses using the leading standardized tests rely upon only a sample of students entering and leaving our institutions, the results of these tests give only a snapshot of learning on a limited set of outcomes at two points in time; and the scores are of little use (and often not reported) to students or faculty. It is surprising, then, that so much attention and reliance is being placed on this thin wire. Significantly, little information from these test results is being used by students or faculty to guide pedagogical and curricular improvements and enhance the quality of teaching and learning. This is a weak strategy. (2009, 3)

Rhodes goes on to explain that VALUE provides information "students can use to self-assess their learning and reflect on their progress. It can inform faculty about what areas of learning, assignments, and pedagogies are effective. And, finally, it can provide a basis for programs, departments, and institutions to showcase student learning (2009).

Data-Gathering Assessment: Bottom-Up Development of a Common Set of Questions

The Consortium for the Study of Writing in College (CSWC), an effort connected with the development and distribution of a set of writing-related questions associated with the National

Survey of Student Engagement (NSSE), is another effort that has potential to speak to questions asked outside and inside the academy about students' experiences with college writing. Unlike the previous two efforts, however, the NSSE is data gathered *from* students—what is often referred to as "indirect" assessment information. But while it does not provide information about students' performances on writing-related work in the same ways that the inter-institutional or VALUE efforts do, it represents an effort driven by writing instructors to gather data that could help to reframe what is meant by "comparability," a key term in public discussions about postsecondary learning.

The CSWC and its set of NSSE writing questions came about when Charles Paine, a composition and rhetoric faculty member at the University of New Mexico, began to wonder whether and how it was possible to add questions to the NSSE. Paine e-mailed the NSSE staff using the "contact" link on their Web site and was electronically introduced to Robert Gonyea, one of NSSE's two associate directors. (Gonyae is the associate director for Research and Data Analysis). After talking with Gonyea, Paine decided to work with the Council of Writing Program Administrators to create a set of writing questions. Paine gathered suggestions for these questions on a listserv, posted them to an interactive wiki for additional feedback, and workshopped them at the CWPA summer conference for two years. They piloted the questions on the 2007 NSSE at eighty-two four-year institutions (the NSSE is intended only for use at four-year institutions; the Community College Survey of Student Engagement, or CCSSE, is used at two-year schools); for the 2008 NSSE, eighty institutions administered the twenty-seven writing-related questions to 27,000 students (Consortium n.d.).

Broadly, questions were grouped in four areas: the strategies students used for writing (e.g., brainstorming, collaboration, receiving feedback, revising, consulting with writing tutors); the kinds of writing assigned (e.g., argumentative, narrative, descriptive, analytical/evaluative, field-specific ["for engineering"]); the kind of information students received from instructors (e.g., directions for writing, explanations of learning or criteria, models of work, feedback on short assignments leading to a longer one, collaboration, discussions about hypothetical or real audiences); and the kinds of finished products students created (e.g., portfolios or pieces for publication).

While the information collected from the CSWC can help writing instructors, program directors, and others on a local campus understand more fully the experience of students (as they are represented by students' responses to the NSSE questions), there may be additional value in the ways the results can help those same instructors and program directors reconceptualize "comparability." As material on the CSWC site explains,

> Participation in the CSWC may be especially helpful for engaging campus administrators in conversations about "comparability." Currently, standards for some measures of comparability exist (e.g., progress toward degree, financial aid awarded, etc.). Information to determine comparability on these measures often comes from the Integrated Postsecondary Education Data System (IPEDS); other information comes from the institution itself.

However, no standards exist for comparability on discipline-specific measures, such as "writing success." This creates an opportunity to proactively shape those standards. Participation in the CSWC will provide campuses with information that can help determine those standards in ways appropriate to the discipline. For instance, campuses can compare themselves to writing programs with similar emphases, campuses that assign similar amounts of writing, campuses whose results are similar, and so forth. Having at hand this kind of nuanced information can help institutions engage in meaningful comparisons that may be used to improve practices (Consortium n.d.).

Like the inter-institutional collaboration and the VALUE efforts, the CSWC represents an effort to develop assessments that speak to concerns about comparable data sets often raised by those outside of programs and institutions. In this way, it also represents an important effort to engage in contemporary assessment discussions, and also represents best practice principles from our discipline.

Prophetic Pragmatism and Reframing

Some might say that efforts like those described in the Pagano et al. article, the AAC&U value project, or the CSWC will not successfully destroy the dominant frame surrounding discussions of education, one associated with business-oriented metaphors and the idea of "college and career readiness." In fact, we agree. And while we might ultimately like to say we should take a more radical stance, defining precisely what *we* want and advocating for that at all costs, we know such a positioning would fall on deaf ears and ultimately cause more harm than good. As we noted in chapters two and four, frames establish boundaries around "what is," around ideas of common sense that reflect and perpetuate larger cultural stories and, importantly, values. And as we discussed in chapter three, members of the academy whose work constitutes part of "higher education" have historically framed that work as a closed system, defining disciplinary boundaries that are strengthened and reinforced by the feedback that they—we— provide to one another through peer review and other mechanisms that reinforce our disciplinary identities. The realities of these frames put in place some very real values and practices that anyone who wants to reframe writing and assessment must consider. Advancing a model for assessment that falls too far outside of this dominant frame could be dismissed out of hand as "unrealistic," "impractical," or worse; adopting a persona in the process of this reframing that is found to be inappropriate or outside of professional boundaries, especially as nontenure-track or untenured instructors, we could be dismissed from our positions all together.

We also must take into account issues of identity related to reframing writing assessment. Within the technocratic frame, assessment is made to seem an impersonal—"objective"—process meant to efficiently gather information about learning, diagnose issues related to that process, and enable prescriptions for problems. To some extent, as members of the academy who participate in the process of boundary-drawing constituted by professional practices like peer review, we also are culpable for perpetuating this frame. But as the scholarship in our field (including this book)—as well as work in aligned fields, like the scholarship of teaching and learning—attests, many understand assessment to be something quite different than the technocratic, efficient process often captured in the term "accountability." In fact, it is integrally tied to the identities and passions of teachers, administrators, and even students, as the inter-institutional, VALUE, and CSWC projects demonstrate.

As we discussed in chapter four, we find the concept of prophetic pragmatism valuable here. The worst thing we can do—for ourselves, for our students, for our institutions, for the worlds in which we live—is to shirk the responsibilities that Professors Chaco and Embler identify, and which we believe (with them) are our responsibilities as literacy educators. To that extent, we also believe that we must understand the dominant frame (and its attendant values and ideologies) and work with it—even within it, if necessary. It's crucial, then, to do what we can, as best we can, while keeping in mind the implications of our actions (for ourselves and others). In the next and final chapter, we will summarize some of the strategies we've discussed here in some important reminders for reframing work.

7

REIMAGINING WRITING ASSESSMENT

Stories matter. Many stories matter. Stories have been used to dispossess and to malign. But stories can also be used to empower.

Chimamanda Adichie
"The Danger of a Single Story" (2009)

Throughout this book, we've discussed the ways that frames and framing shape individual and group perceptions of what is "commonsensical" and what is outside of the boundaries of "common sense." From communication studies and linguistics (Carey 1989; Hall 1983; Hanks 1995; Ryan 1991), to literature and literary criticism (Adichie 2009; Faulkner [in Wise 1980]; Ondajte 1996; Williams 1973), to historiography (Wise 1980; White 1978), a variety of authors and texts allude to the same point: in a circular and self-referential way, frames reflect and perpetuate stories, and the process of framing influences how we tell and interpret those tales. These stories, in turn, shape experiences, perceptions of the world, and values and beliefs, reinforcing the frames that gave shape to the stories in the beginning. Dominant frames and stories become "common sense" and naturalized so that we often aren't able to see them for what they are; in the process, they also come to represent the dominant values and ideologies associated with and perpetuated by the frame.

In the early years of the twenty-first century, we see this process at work in stories about education and teachers. The idea that college and career readiness is the primary purpose of school, for instance, is becoming the dominant frame through

which stories about education are told. Stories about or referring to "college and career readiness" are linked to a number
of other tales about what school is or isn't or what students are
or aren't doing, almost like a painting composed of overlap-
ping layers.

The first layer consists of ubiquitous tales about the need
to continually prepare America's youth to participate in the
advancement of the democracy (and, in fact, the notion that
the nation is a steadily advancing democracy), a story rooted in
the nation's foundational stories about itself (Bercovitch 1978;
Noble 1985). On top of this are other stories that have circu-
lated through American culture for the last 150 plus years: about
how American dominance associated with economic power has
shifted away from the United States; about how new forms of
technology are enabling the circulation of values and ideals that
seem questionable (or threatening or detrimental, depending
on one's perspective) to the advancement of knowledge in the
democracy; about how students aren't learning "what they need
to" as a result of these factors; about how teachers and schools,
out of touch with reality, aren't able to significantly affect what
students know (Fallows 2010; for more on the perpetual "crisis"
in education, also see Berliner and Biddle 1995).

In the early years of the twentieth century, these stories were
closely associated with developments in communication technology. The telegraph, the train, the car, the radio, and the
motion picture were (rightly) believed to have hastened the
movement of ideas (and values) rapidly around a vast nation
that had previously existed as sort of loosely connected, relatively autonomous cities and states (Czitrom 1983; Susman
1984). What Warren Susman calls "the rapid accumulation
of both new knowledge and new experiences" made possible
by these technologies seemed to stand in stark contrast to
the sense of isolated community that many perceived to have
existed before the "communication revolution" (for a secondary analysis of this phenomenon see Susman 1984 or West 1989,
for instance). Among the products of this tension between "old"

and "new" were attempts by intellectuals to equip American citizens to deal with the flood of new information and ideas available to them—to emphasize, for instance, the importance of a citizenry equipped with method, "techniques specifically developed to deal with the reality that all seemed so anxious to touch, to understand, to use" (Susman 1984, 111). These techniques included strategies to identify and address challenges that would arise as a result of access to new information "naturally" being taught in school. The primary point of debate about education during this turn-of-the-century period was not, in fact, whether students should learn these methods, but what the best approach was to helping them do so (Adler-Kassner 2008; West 1984). There is a relationship, then, between the instructional approaches and assessment methodologies discussed in chapters two and three and the real and perceived changes occurring in the United States during this period.

Flashing forward 110 years, the rapid movement of ideas and, now, economies continues to be an important undercurrent beneath frames surrounding education and stories about what school should be. The fever pitch at which these stories are told leads "logically" to the need for a fast solution. Education is failing, they say—failing to prepare students, failing to close the "achievement gap," failing to make sure the nation stays on course—because standards are too low, or students and teachers aren't held accountable. This can be accomplished by standardizing the K-12 educational system so that there is one single story of what high school diploma (and, perhaps in the future, a college degree) means. This will ensure that students will come to college with a shared level of preparation – the "common inputs" described by Shamila Basu Conger and Christine Tell (2007) discussed in chapter six – which will, in turn, presumably enable college educators to build upon that standard foundation in ways that will move students forward along the assembly line of education to career readiness. This story is told and retold in reports such as *Ready or Not, A Test of Leadership,* and *Accountability for Greater Results.* At the K-12 level, it is codified in documents such as the Common Core State Standards Initiative whose adoption is linked to states' eligibility to apply for Race to the Top funding (see Common Core State Standards Initiative and Social Studies, for instance). It is reinforced at all levels of the curriculum by assessments that are benchmarked to externally established standards, such as those associated with the MAAP, the CAPP, or the CLA. Agree with our story, conform to it, these mandates or directives say, and you can be labeled successful; resist our standards and you fail. The dominant metaphor in this story comes from business-oriented practices that emphasize the production of consistent inputs and outputs developed through Total Quality Management.

RE-SEEING WRITING ASSESSMENT: A DIFFERENT TALE

In identifying this frame and these stories, we do not want to suggest that there are *not* issues to be addressed in education. Those with progressive and conservative views alike can easily point with alarm to differences in the rates of college placement and persistence by members of different socioeconomic groups. For example, regardless of what one thinks of standardized assessments like the National Assessment of Educational Progress (NAEP), the most respected of the national assessments used in K–12 schools, the gap in scores between white students and African American and Hispanic students persists (though NAEP data also show an increase in reading scores for all students, and a sharper rise in those scores for Hispanic and, especially, African American students over the last forty years [National Center for Education Statistics n.d.]). There's no doubt but that now, as always, there *are* issues to be addressed in the school system—as there are in the broader culture, as well.

What we *do* mean to suggest is that college writing instructors and program directors need to have a hand in helping to shape the many layers of narrative that contribute to the overall shape of these stories. Currently, in the policy discourse, one story—that about college and career readiness—is being repeated over and over again. Of course, as we note in chapter six, there are even alternatives within that frame—Achieve/ADP and the AAC&U both make the case that education should prepare students for careers; they just define the terms associated with "readiness" very differently. But there are less dominant frames circulating as well, such as the positions being advanced by groups like the Common Core, a group that includes educational policy experts like Diane Ravitch; these experts are arguing for "challenging, rigorous instruction in the full range of liberal arts and sciences" in order to foster flexible, creative, and inquisitive thinkers (Common Core, n.d.). Then there are stories told by teachers and researchers reflected in documents like the NCTE Beliefs about the Teaching of Writing (National Council 2004), or the work of individual instructors and programs like the ones we included in chapter five—stories about real students engaged in actual classroom work and how their learning was improved based on the efforts of dedicated teachers involved in teaching and assessment as research. To promote these alternative stories, we must contribute to—even help to change—the layers of meaning that surround stories about this work.

Metaphors and Models for Practice: Honeycombs or Networked Infrastructures

Successful reframing effort involves creating a conceivable model—what George Lakoff summarizes as a metaphor (2004)—for assessment grounded in a track record of content and practice (Nunberg 2006). We can't emphasize this latter point enough—story-changing is more than just window dressing through language (what those outside of our field pejoratively refer to as "just rhetoric")—it requires simultaneously conceptualizing, acting upon, and representing work thoughtfully grounded in research, method, and practices. Throughout this book, we have also suggested that these models must be designed and built collaboratively, with careful attention to the values and passions of all involved, through a process that provides access to all. Once we have considered all these issues, only *then* can we move from them to consider metaphors and models for what reframing writing assessment might look like in order to make this process conceivable for ourselves and for others.

In considering alternative metaphors, we are also mindful of what we believe, following David Shupe (2008) and Lynn Priddy (2009), to be the fundamental (assessment) challenge facing postsecondary educators in the twenty-first century: the need to develop not only meaningful dialogue between those who understand assessment as a process for improving student learning and those who are concerned with making sure education is "accountable," but also fostering understandings of the conceptual positions that make these different perspectives on what is necessary possible. This work requires careful listening, a level of understanding that probably approaches empathy, and a commitment to shared action that must be supported within academic disciplines, by academic institutions, and by those outside the academy, often referred to as "stakeholders," who are invested in what students learn in college.

With these caveats in mind, we have arrived at two possibilities that might be starting places for developing different metaphors for education, metaphors that lead to different implications and practices. Both of these reflect the kind of work being undertaken through efforts like the Pagano et. al. (2008) pilot project and AAC&U's VALUE initiative, as well as work like Haswell's book *Beyond Outcomes* (2001), Huot's *(Re)Articulating Writing Assessment* (2002), Bob Broad's *What We Really Value* (2003), Bob Broad et al.'s *Organic Writing Assessment* (2009), Patricia Lynne's *Coming to Terms* (2004), and other texts that have attempted to provide not only critiques of existing assessment models, but frameworks and language for new approaches to this work.

Assessment as Honeycomb

The first potential alternative metaphor is *assessment as honeycomb*. Here, individual disciplines define the boundaries of their practice and determine at the local level questions to be studied, methods for analysis, and uses of data. As with real honeycombs, this model for assessment is dependent on an internally cohesive structure. If one cell is not strong—that is, if one discipline or area that defines itself as a site for assessment is not defined clearly and supported by a boundary defining it as separate from others—the entire structure is that much weaker. But within this model (as in a honeycomb), the individual cells also have to look pretty much alike—that is, they must be the same size, possess the same dimensions, and link together successfully in order to form a cohesive whole. This might lead to an approach to assessment, then, in which a uniform model based in the institution (this *particular* honeycomb) is developed for assessing student learning, and that model might (or might not) take into account particular disciplinary principles and practices. Additionally, the overall frame for the honeycomb—the borders that serve as the outside boundaries of the frame in which it is built—would necessarily be constructed outside the individual cells.

Extending from the metaphor of the honeycomb leads to some concepts that might resonate with current practices: a honeycomb is organic, it changes, it is built by a collective collaboration among a number of individuals, it serves a distinct purpose (it is not built just for the sake of building). It is also affected by local conditions—the type of flowers the honey is made from, for instance. Then again, it also may extend to features that might not resonate as effectively with some instructors' or program directors' values: there are queen bees and worker bees in the colony for which the honeycomb is constructed, the worker bees' roles are to work tirelessly for the queen, and often the by-product of the honeycomb, the honey itself, is used for purposes other than those directly benefitting the colony that created it.

Assessment as Networked Infrastructure

A second possible metaphor representing approaches to assessment might be an *information infrastructure*. This concept, which draws on work by Jeff Grabill (2007), information strategists like John Seely Brown (e.g., Brown and Duguid 2000), and framing analysis as described in chapter two, refers to a loosely networked group of alliances that is fairly flexible. Grabill's work on information infrastructures provides the broad outline for the concept as we define it, as he moves "information" away from a model that defines it as a commodity developed by one entity and transmitted to another (2007, 23–26). Instead, Grabill says, information is "most likely an artifact . . . but it is purposeful, linked, and interconnected, and part of a web of other resources" (27). Infrastructures emerge from temporal processes and are sometimes manifested in a series of physical structures that shape understandings of and possibilities for information, processes, and structures that themselves reflect particular values and ideologies and sometimes create boundaries for perpetuating them (27–31). As Grabill conceptualizes them, then, "infrastructures are designed and given meaning and value within specific contexts (communities, people, tasks). Contingent and designed, infrastructures nonetheless enact, sometimes rigorously, a set of standards . . . making their design a crucial site of intellectual and political activity" (30–31).

Within this concept of the information infrastructure, assessment work becomes at once more specific to the particular context—institutional, student, and discipline—and more immediately relevant to concerns for civic action. Each point in the infrastructure is responsible for defining its boundaries, identifying goals central to its work, outlining processes for studying the extent to which those goals are reached (how, why, and so on), and what will happen as a result of the study. But while this metaphor for assessment strongly privileges the construction of strong individual (and loosely networked) nodes within the infrastructure, it also invokes a more loosely connected, flexibly constructed model of external boundaries than does the honeycomb. It might seem more appealing, then, to those who favor strong local control and work with internal audiences (e.g., disciplinary instructors), but would perhaps not speak to those who see a need for large-scale data that speak to external audiences. Similarly, like the honeycomb, the information infrastructure extends to some ideas that might resonate with current practices: it builds from information, it is constructed from the inside, and the connections from it extend outward. At the same time, it also extends to values and ideas that might not speak as clearly to writing studies professionals. At its root, the idea of information infrastructure is rooted in business, and invokes the concept of information that can be easily transmitted from one place to another. A network also could invoke the concept of a net, something meant to catch or capture things that go awry.

Of course, these are just two possible metaphors through which we might reconceptualize and reframe writing assessment—and there are many more that might be equally or more effective for this work. Each, however, relies on the central processes of reframing that we have stressed throughout this book: thinking about the frames surrounding contemporary discussions of education and their historical roots; working strategically (by building alliances, developing strategies with others, and communicating effectively with audiences outside and inside the academy) about writing and about assessment processes; and considering how we frame (or want to reframe) our efforts within the broader context of contemporary discussions about assessment. It is helpful, too, to remember that like all things, this is a process. Reframing is never done, but together we can participate in ongoing discussions to continually contribute to a frame that keeps improving student learning squarely in the center.

TAKING ACTION: ESSENTIAL TIPS FOR REFRAMING WRITING ASSESSMENT

We conclude with what we hope will become an ever-growing "quick" reference list (inasmuch as any piece of academic writing is ever "quick") for reframing writing assessment based on the analysis and stories in this book.

Use rhetorical skills to construct frames and tell different stories. As writing teachers and composition and rhetoric scholars, we understand that concepts such as audience, purpose and genre need to guide our discourse if we are going to be effective. Unfortunately, as Mike Rose notes (2010), we are so steeped in our disciplinary language and context that we have trouble writing and communicating with nonacademic audiences about our scholarship. For some specific help about how to do this in reference to issues related to writing, try the Council of Writing Program Administrator's Assessment Gallery, which has a variety of resources such as the NCTE-CWPA *White Paper on Writing Assessment* and a convenient reference on strategies for discussing assessment and writing instruction (http://wpacouncil.org/assessment-gallery). CWPA also sponsors the Network for Media Action (NMA), which creates frameworks for talking about specific writing related issues, such as machine scoring and the SAT/ACT writing sections (http://wpacouncil.org/nma). NMA sponsors the National Conversation on Writing, a participatory multi-media project that aims "to gather person-by-person accounts of people's everyday experiences with writing" (http://ncow.org/site).

"Get involved," as Professor Chaco suggests, in education issues beyond your department and campus boundaries. This could be as simple as responding to an editorial in the local newspaper or attending an open forum at a local public school or community group to "plant seeds," as Professor Embler puts it. Getting involved might also include serving on Department of Education committees at the state level or as part of a national commission. Serving in these venues makes a valuable contribution to how writing pedagogy and assessment are understood and provides opportunities to influence policies. However, as we hear from Professors Chaco and Embler, it also means being willing to learn from the other participants and negotiate, keeping in mind the long view.

W/o getting involued no, change can occur!

Approach writing assessment as a scholarly endeavor. We need to use our knowledge and expertise as a scholars to do assessment (O'Neill, Schendel, and Huot 2002) as we saw in some of the case studies in chapter four. Through this approach, we can articulate questions for study, define appropriate methods, collect data systematically, and contextualize your work within a disciplinary framework. This approach also provides opportunities to publish findings and contribute to the ongoing scholarly conversation about writing assessment, contributions valued by departments and institutions.

Value community-based work and support faculty who do it. Getting involved—at the local, state, and national levels—can be very time demanding. As Professor Chaco says, getting involved with one project leads to others. It can require devoting our limited time to activities usually defined as "service." Professor Embler suggests working within institutions to make sure this kind of service is considered part of the scholarly work academics are required to do. Community-based work is a form of dissemination of scholarship and relies on one's disciplinary expertise. While not everyone is adept at this kind of work, we can support colleagues who do it by making sure it is recognized and rewarded.

Build alliances with others on campus, in the community, or in cyber-scace. Local collaborations might include English education colleagues, secondary English teachers, or community college faculty. More extensive networking might involve joining national discussion groups such as the wcenters (see this link for information on joining http://writingcenters.org/resources/starting-a-writing-cente/#Mail) or WPA-L (https://lists.asu.edu/cgi-bin/wa?A0=WPA-L). Collaboration can take many forms: joining or starting an official group, such as a local affiliate of the Council of Writing Program Administrators or other professional organizations; working with the local National Writing Project site; or creating an informal network with other writing faculty from local institutions. Joining with others in similar institutions, in a national network, as composition and rhetoric faculty in Jesuit colleges as universities have done, can be useful (see the Jesuit Conference on Rhetoric and Composition at http://bellarmine.lmu.edu/english/pubs/jcrc.htm). Even incorporating writing-related service learning into a writing course can be a way to build relationships with others around writing pedagogy and assessment (and it can help "plant seeds" for harvesting later when issues related to writing crop up in public fora).

Realize that this work is never done. As good teachers, we never think a class is perfect, something we'll never change again. We need to realize, as we do about teaching, that neither assessment nor reframing is ever completed. As teachers and as researchers, some of our most valuable and exciting insights came when we heard, read, saw, or otherwise took in something that rocked the foundations of what we believed, our perceptions on a particular issue, or our understandings of something or other. These are the "aha!" moments we hope students will reach in their writing, after all. In the same way, we need to understand that if we approach writing assessment and reframing as genuine participants, we will continue to learn, to grow, to say, "aha!" And after all—isn't that why we do this work?

Continue to learn about reframing and contribute to the efforts. Participate – or continue to participate – in conversations with colleagues, administrators, and even students about writing instruction and assessment on the local level. At the national level, get involved! Organizations like the Council of Writing Program Administrators (WPA), the Conference on College Composition and Communication (CCCC), the International Writing Centers Association (IWCA), the Two-Year College Association (TYCA), and the National Council of Teachers of English (NCTE) have multiple opportunities for instructors and program directors to participate – check them out! And remember... reframing writing assessment, like writing, is a process that improves with revision and practice.

REFERENCES

Achieve. 2004. *Ready or not: Creating a high school diploma that counts.* American Diploma Project. www.achieve.org/ReadyorNot.

———. 2008. *Measures that matter: Making college and career readiness the mission for high schools: A guide for state policymakers. The Education Trust.* http://www. achieve.org/node/1048.

———. 2009. *Closing the expectations gap 2009: Fourth annual 50-state progress report on the alignment of high school policies with the demands of college and careers.* http://www.achieve.org/closingtheexpectationsgap2009.

———. 2010. Achieve.org.

Adichie, Chimamanda. 2009. *The danger of a single story.* http://www.ted.com/ talks/chimamanda_adichie_the_danger_of_a_single_story.html.

Adelman, Chad, and Kevin Carey. 2009. *Ready to assemble: Grading state higher education accountability systems. Education Sector.* http://www.educationsector. org/.

Adler-Kassner, Linda. 2008. *The activist WPA: Changing stories about writers and writing.* Logan: Utah State University Press.

———. 2010. The WPA as activist: Systematic strategies for framing, action, and representation. In Rose and Weiser.

——— and Susanmarie Harrington. 2009. Reframing the accountability debate. *Inside Higher Education.* http://www.insidehighered.com/ views/2009/04/23/adler.

——— n.d. Responsibility and composition's future in the twenty-first century: Reframing "accountability." *College Composition and Communication.* Forthcoming.

Agnew, Eleanor, and Margaret McLauglin. 1999. Basic writing class of '93 five years later: How the academic paths of blacks and whites diverged. *Journal of Basic Writing* 18 (1): 40–54.

———. 2001. Those crazy gates and how they swing: Tracking the system that tracks African-American students. In *Mainstreaming Basic Writers Politics and Pedagogies of Access,* eds. Gerri McNenny and Sallyanne H. Fitzgerald. Mahwah, NJ: Lawrence Erlbaum Associates.

Alinsky, Saul. 1946. *Reveille for radicals.* New York: Vintage.

Allen, Michael. 1995. Valuing differences: Portnet's first year. *Assessing Writing* 2: 67–90.

Aliamo, Peter J., John C. Bean, Joseph M. Langenhan, and Larry Nichols. 2009. Eliminating lab reports: A rhetorical approach for teaching the scientific paper in sophomore organic chemistry. *WAC Journal* 20 (Nov): 17-32

American Council on Education. 2008. *ACE analysis of Higher Education Act reauthorization.* www.acenet.edu/e-newsletters/p2p/ACE_HEA_analysis_818.pdf.

American Educational Research Association, American Psychological Association, and National Council on Measurement in Education. 1999.

Standards for Educational and Psychological Testing. Washington, DC: American Educational Research Association.

Anson, Chris M. 2008. The intelligent design of writing programs: Reliance on belief or a future of evidence. *WPA Journal* 32 (1): 11–36.

———. 2009. Closed systems and standardized writing tests. *College Composition and Communication* 60: 113–127.

Apple, Michael. 1979. *Ideology and curriculum.* London: Routledge and Kegan Paul.

Applebee, Arthur N. 1986. Problems in process approaches: Toward a reconceptualization of process instruction. In *The teaching of writing: Eighty-fifth yearbook of the National Society for the Study of Education, Part II,* eds. Anthony R. Petrosky and David Bartholomae. Chicago: University of Chicago Press.

Association of American Colleges and Universities (AAC&U). 2007. *College learning for the new global century.* Washington DC: AAC&U.

———. 2009. VALUE: *Valid assessment of learning in undergraduate education initiative.* http://www.aacu.org/value/rubrics/index_p.cfm.

Ball, Arnetha. 1997. Expanding the dialogue on culture as a critical component when assessing writing. *Assessing Writing* 4:169–202.

——— and Ted Lardner. 1997. Dispositions toward language: Teacher constructs of knowledge and the Ann Arbor Black English case. *College Composition and Communication* 48: 469–485.

——— and Pamela Ellis. 2008. Identity and the writing of culturally and linguistically diverse students. In *Handbook of research on writing: History, society, school, individual, text,* ed. Charles Bazerman. New York: Lawrence Erlbaum Associates.

Bawarshi, Anis. 2003. *Genre and the invention of the writer.* Logan: Utah State University Press.

Bazerman, Charles. 2004. Speech acts, genres, and activity systems: How texts organize activity and people. In *What writing does and how it does it: An introduction to analyzing texts and textual practices,* eds. Charles Bazerman and Paul A. Prior. Mahwah, NJ: Erlbaum.

Bean, John C., David Carrithers, and Theresa Earenfight. 2005. Transforming WAC through a discourse-based approach to university outcomes assessment. *WAC Journal* 16: 5–21.

Belanoff, Pat, and Peter Elbow. 1986. Using portfolios to increase collaboration and community in a writing program. *Writing Program Administration* 9 (3): 27–40.

Bender, Thomas. 1993. *Intellect and public life.* Baltimore: Johns Hopkins University Press.

Berieter, Carl, and Marlene Scardamalia. 1987. *The psychology of written composition.* Hillsdale, NJ: Erlbaum.

Berliner, David, and Bruce Biddle. 1995. *The manufactured crisis: Myths, fraud, and the attack on America's public schools.* New York: Perseus.

Bercovitch, Savcan. 1978. *The American jeremiad.* Madison: University of Wisconsin Press.

Berkenkotter, Carol, Thomas N. Huckin, and John Ackerman. 1991. Social context and socially constructed texts: The initiation of a graduate student into a writing research community. In *Textual dynamics of the professions:*

Historical and contemporary studies of writing in professional communities, eds. Charles Bazerman and James Paradis. Madison: University of Wisconsin Press.

Bizzell, Patricia, and Bruce Herzberg, eds. 1990. *The Rhetorical tradition: Readings from classical times to the present.* Boston: Bedford St. Martin's.

Black, Laurel, Donald A. Daiker, Jeffrey Sommers, and Gail Stygall, eds. 1994. *New directions in portfolio assessment: Reflective practice, critical theory, and large-scale scoring.* Portsmouth, NH: Boynton/Cook Heinemann.

Bolman, Lee, and Terence Deal. 2003. *Reframing organizations: Artistry, choice, and leadership.* San Francisco: Jossey-Bass.

Borrowman, Shane. 1999. The trinity of portfolio placement: Validity, reliability, and curriculum Reform. *WPA: Writing Program Administration* 23 (1/2): 7–28.

Boyte, Harry. 2005. Reframing democracy: Governance, civic agency, and politics. *Public Administration Review* 65. Accessed from http://www.hhh.umn.edu/centers/cdc/research.html.

Bray, Robert. 2000. *Spin works!* San Francisco: SPIN Project.

Brennan, Robert L., ed. 2006. *Educational measurement, 4th edition.* Westport, CT: American Council on Education/Praeger.

Brereton, John C., ed. 1995. *The origins of composition studies in the American college 1875-1925: A documentary history.* Pittsburgh: University of Pittsburgh Press.

Broad, Bob. 2000. Pulling your hair out: Crises of standardization in communal writing assessment. *Research in the Teaching of English.* 35: 213–60.

Broad, Bob. 2003. *What we really value: Beyond rubrics in teaching and assessing writing.* Logan: Utah State University Press.

———, Linda Adler-Kassner, Barry Alford, et al. 2009. *Organic writing assessment: Dynamic criteria mapping in action.* Logan: Utah State University Press.

Broad, Robert L. 1994. "Portfolio scoring": A contradiction in terms. In Black et al., 263–77.

Bruffee, Kenneth. 1986. Beginning a testing program: Making lemonade. In *Writing assessment: Issues and strategies*, eds. Karen L. Greenberg, Harvey S. Weiner, and Richard A. Donovan. New York: Longman.

Burke, Kenneth. 1966. *Language as symbolic action.* University of California Press.

Callahan, Susan. 1997. Tests worth taking?: Using portfolios for accountability in Kentucky. *Research in the Teaching of English* 31: 295–336.

Camp, Roberta. 1993. Changing the model for the direct assessment of writing. In Williamson and Huot.

Carey, James. 1978. A plea for the university tradition. *Journalism Quarterly* 55 (4): 846–855.

———. 1989. *Communication as culture.* New York: Routledge.

———. 1997. The press, public opinion, and public discourse. In *James Carey: A critical reader*, eds. Eve Stryker Munson and Catherine A. Warren. Minneapolis: University of Minnesota Press.

Carrithers, David, and John C. Bean. 2008. Using a client memo to assess critical thinking of finance majors. *Business Communication Quarterly* 71 (1): 10–26.

Carrithers, David, Teresa Ling, and John C. Bean. 2008. Messy problems and lay audiences: Teaching critical thinking in the finance curriculum. *Business Communication Quarterly* 71 (2): 152–70.

Carter, Michael. 2003. A process for establishing outcomes-based assessment plans for writing and speaking in the disciplines. *Language and Learning Across the Disciplines* 6 (1). http://wac.colostate.edu/llad/v6n1/carter.pdf.

Cazden, Courtney. 2001. *Classroom discourse: The language of teaching and learning.* 2nd ed. Portsmouth, NH: Heinemann.

Cherry, Roger, and Paul Meyer. 1993. Reliability issues in holistic assessment. In Williamson and Huot.

Cohen, Geoffrey L., Claude M. Steele, and Lee D. Ross. 1999. The mentor's dilemma; Providing critical feedback across the racial divide. *Personality and Social Psychology Bulletin* 25: 1302–18.

Condon, William, and Diane Kelly-Riley. 2004. Assessing and teaching what we value: The relationship between college-level writing and critical thinking abilities. *Assessing Writing* 9: 56–75.

Common Core State Standards Initiative. n.d. National Governors Association and Council of Chief State School Officers. .http://www.corestandards.org/.

Conference on College Composition and Communication. 2006. *Writing assessment: A position statement.* http://www.ncte.org/cccc/resources/positions/123784.htm.

Conger, Sharmila Basu, and Christine Tell. 2007. Curriculum and assessment systems. In *More student success: A systemic solution.* Boulder, CO: State Higher Education Executive Officers.

Connors, Robert J. 1997. *Composition-rhetoric: Backgrounds, theory, and pedagogy.* Pittsburgh: University of Pittsburgh Press.

Consortium for the Study of Writing in College. n.d. *Frequently asked questions about the NSSE Consortium for the Study of Writing in College.* http://comppile.org/wpa+nsse/faq/index.htm.

Cook-Gumperz, Jenny. 2006. *The social construction of literacy.* 2nd ed. Cambridge, UK: Cambridge University Press.

Council of Writing Program Administrators. 2008. *Assessment Gallery.* http://wpacouncil.org/assessment-gallery.

Cronbach, Lee J. 1988. Five perspectives on validity argument. In *Test validity,* eds. Howard Wainer and Henry Braun. Hillsdale: Laurence Erlbaum.

———. 1989. Construct validation after thirty years. In *Intelligence measurement, theory and public policy: Proceedings of a symposium in honor of L. G. Humphreys,* ed. Robert L. Linn. Urbana: University of Illinois Press.

Crow, Steve. 2007. Maintaining focus through the challenges of accountability. Foundations of Excellence keynote address. http://www.fyfoundations.org/pdf/Oakton Address_SteveCrow_April 2007.pdf.

Crowley, Sharon. 1998. *Composition in the university: Historical and polemical essays.* Pittsburgh: University of Pittsburgh Press.

Cuban, Larry. 2004. *The blackboard and the bottom line: Why schools can't be businesses.* Cambridge: Harvard University Press.

Czitrom, Daniel. 1983. *Media and the American mind: From Morse to McLuhan.* Chapel Hill: University of North Carolina Press.

Daiker, Donald A., Jeffrey Sommers, and Gail Stygall. 1996. The pedagogical implications of a college placement portfolio. In *Assessment of writing: Politics, policies, practice,* eds. Edward M. White, William D. Lutz, and Sandra Kamusikiri, New York: MLA.

Darling-Hammond, Linda. 2004. Standards, accountability, and school reform. *Teachers College Record* 106 (6): 1047–1085.

Decker, Emily, George Cooper, and SusanMarie Harrington. (1993). Crossing institutional boundaries: Developing an entrance portfolio assessment to improve writing instruction. *Journal of Teaching Writing* 12, 83-104.

Delli Carpini, Dominic. 2004. *Composing a life's work: Writing, citizenship, and your occupation.* New York: Pearson.

Diederich, Paul B. 1974. *Measuring growth in English.* Urbana, IL: National Council of Teachers of English.

Diederich, Paul B., John W. French, and Sydell T. Carlton. 1961. *Factors in judgments of writing quality.* Princeton: Educational Testing Service.

Douglas, Wallace. 1976. Rhetoric of the meritocracy: The creation of composition at Harvard. In *English in the American university: A radical view of the profession,* ed. Richard Ohmann. Hanover, NH: University Press of New England.

Durst, Russel K. 1999. *Collision course: Conflict, negotiation, and learning in college composition.* Urbana, IL: National Council of Teachers of English.

Edwonkette. 2008. It's a small world after all. http://blogs.edweek.org/edweek/eduwonkette/2008/02/its_a_small_world_after_all_1.html.

Elbow, Peter. 2000. Premises and foundations. In *Everyone can write,* ed. Peter Elbow. New York: Oxford University Press.

Elbow, Peter, and Pat Belanoff. 1986a. Staffroom interchange: Portfolios as a substitute for proficiency examinations. *College Composition and Communication* 37: 336–39.

———. 1986b. State University of New York, Stony Brook. In *New methods in college writing programs: Theories in practice,* eds. Paul Connolly and Teresa Vilardi, New York: Modern Language Association.

Elliot, Norbert. 2005. *On a Scale: A social history of writing assessment in America.* New York: Peter Lang.

Fallows, James. 2010. How can America rise again? *The Atlantic* January/February: 38–55.

Flower, Linda and John Hayes. 1980. The cognition of discovery: Defining a rhetorical problem. *College Composition and Communication.* 31 (1): 21-32.

———. 1981. A cognitive process theory of writing. *College Composition and Communication* 32: 365–387.

Fulkerson, Richard. 2005. Composition at the turn of the 21st century. *College Composition and Communication* 56: 654–687.

Ganz, Marshall. 2001. The power of story in social movements. Paper prepared for the Annual Meeting of the American Sociological Association, Anaheim, CA. . http://www.lokman.org/2009/04/01/marshall-ganz-on-narrative-and-social-movements.

Garan, Elaine. 2005. Scientific flim-flam: A who's who of entrepreneurial research. In *Reading for profit: How the bottom line leaves kids behind.* Ed. Bess Altwerger. Portsmouth: Heinemann.

Gee, James Paul. 1996. *Social linguistics and literacies: Ideology in discourses.* 2nd ed. London: Taylor and Francis.

Gere, Anne Ruggles. 1980. Written composition: Toward a theory of evaluation. *College English* 42: 44–48, 53–58.

Godshalk, Fred I., Frances Swineford, and William E. Coffman. 1966. *The measurement of writing ability.* Princeton, NJ: Educational Testing Service. CEEB RM No. 6.

Grabill, Jeffrey. 2007. *Writing community change: Designing technologies for citizen action.* Creskill, NJ: Hampton Press.

Gramsci, Antonio. 1985. *Selections from cultural writings,* eds. David Forgacs and Geoffrey Nowell-Smith. Translated by William Boelhower. London: Lawrence and Wishart.

Green, Angela. 2009. The politics of literacy: Countering the rhetoric of accountability in the Spellings Report and beyond. *College Composition and Communication* 61: W367–W384.

Greenberg, Karen L. 1998. Grading, evaluating, assessing: Power and politics in college composition. *College Composition and Communication* 49: 275–84.

Haertel, Edward H. 2006. Reliability. In Brennan.

Hall, Stuart. 1983. The narrative construction of reality. *Context.* http://www.dalkeyarchive.com/article/show/31.

Hanks, William. 1995. *Language and communicative practices.* Boulder, CO: Westview Press.

Hansen, Kristine. 2005. Religious freedom in the public square and the composition classroom. In VanderLie and Kyburz.

Harris, Muriel. 1999. Diverse research methodology at work for diverse audiences: Shaping the writing center to the institution. In *The writing program administrator as researcher,* eds. Shirley Rose and Irwin Weiser. Portsmouth, NH: Boynton/Cook.

Haswell, Richard H. 1998. Multiple inquiry into the validation of writing tests. *Assessing Writing* 5: 89–110.

———. ed. 2001. *Beyond outcomes: Assessment and instruction within a university writing program.* Vol. 5, Perspectives on Writing Theory, Research and Practice. Westport, CT: Ablex.

———. 2005. NCTE/CCCC's recent war on scholarship. *Written Communication* 22 (2): 198–223.

———. 2005a. Postsecondary entrance writing placement. http://comppile.tamucc.edu/placement.htm.

———, and Janis Tedesco Haswell. 1996. Gender bias and critique of student writing. *Assessing Writing* 3: 31–84.

———, and Susan Wyche-Smith. 1994. Adventuring into writing assessment. *College Composition and Communication* 45: 220–36.

Hawthorne, Joan. 2006. Approaching assessment as if it matters. In *The writing center director's resource book,* eds. Christina Murphy and Byron Stay. Mahwah, NJ: Erlbaum.

Hayes, John R., and Jill A. Hatch. 1999. Issues in measuring reliability: Correlation versus percentage of agreement. *Written Communication* 16: 354–67.

Heath, Shirley Brice. 1983. *Ways with words: Language, life, and work in communities and classrooms.* Cambridge, UK: Cambridge University Press.

Herrington, Anne and Marcia Curtis. 2000. *Persons in process: Four stories of writing and personal development in college.* Urbana: National Council of Teachers of English.

Hertog, James, and Douglas McLeod. 2001. A multiperspectival approach to framing analysis: A field guide. In *Framing public life*, eds. Stephen D. Reese, Oscar H. Gandy, and August E. Grant. Mahway, NJ: Lawrence Erlbaum.

Hester, Vicki, Peggy O'Neill, Michael Neal, Anthony Edgington, and Brian Huot. 2007. Adding portfolios to the placement process: A longitudinal perspective. In O'Neill.

Hillocks, George. 2002. *The testing trap: How state writing assessments control learning*. New York: Teachers College Press.

Horner, Winifred. 1990. The roots of modern writing instruction: Eighteenth- and nineteenth-century Britain. *Rhetoric Review* 8 (2): 322–345.

Hull, Glynda, and Mike Rose. 1990. "This wooden shack place": The logic of an unconventional reading. *College Composition and Communication* 41: 287–98.

Hull, Glynda, Mike Rose, Kay Losey Fraser, and Marisa Castellano. 1991. Remediation as social construct: Perspectives from an analysis of classroom discourse. *College Composition and Communication* 42: 299–329.

Huot, Brian. 1990. The literature of direct writing assessment: Major concerns and prevailing trends. *Review of Educational Research* 60: 237–63.

———. 1993. The influence of holistic scoring procedures on reading and rating student essays. In Williamson and Huot.

———. 2002. *(Re)Articulating writing assessment for teaching and learning*. Logan: Utah State University Press.

———. 2007. Consistently inconsistent: Business and the Spellings Commission report on higher education. *College English* 69: 512–525.

——— and Michael Neal. 2006. Writing assessment: A techno-history. In *Handbook of writing research,* eds. C. A. MacArthur, S. Graham, and J. Fitzgerald, New York: Guilford Press.

Huot, Brian, and Peggy O'Neill, eds. 2009. *Assessing writing: A critical sourcebook*. Boston: Bedford St. Martins.

Johanek, Cindy. 2000. *Composing research: A contextualist paradigm for rhetoric and composition*. Logan: Utah State University Press.

Jones, Diane Auer. 2009. Higher education assessment: Who are we assessing, and for what purpose? *Peer Review* 11 (1): 35.

Kane, Michael T. 2006. Validation. In Brennan.

Kells, Michele Hall. 2007. Writing across communities: Deliberation and the discursive possibilities of WAC. *Reflections* 11 (1): 87–108.

Kitzhaber, Albert R. 1990. *Rhetoric in American colleges, 1850–1900*. Dallas: Southern Methodist University Press.

Klein, Alyson. 2010. Obama budget calls for major shifts on ESEA. *Education Week*. http://www.edweek.org/ew/articles/2010/02/01/21budget_ep.h29.html?tkn=STYFo3Lpq3b0hbjW1iHtq3HWkxWULDI1hdrY.

Krugman, Paul. 2009. How did economists get it so wrong? *New York Times Magazine*, September 6. http://www.nytimes.com/2009/09/06/magazine/06Economic-t.html.

Labaree, David. 1997. Public goods, private goods: The American struggle over educational goals. *American Educational Research Journal* 34 (1): 39–81.

———. 2007. *Education, markets, and the public good*. London: Routledge.

Lakoff, George. 2004. *Don't think of an elephant! Know your values and frame the debate*. White River Junction, VT: Chelsea Green.

————. 2006. *Thinking points: Communicating our American values and visions.* New York: Farrar, Straus and Giroux.

Lederman, Doug. 2007. Explaining the accreditation debate. *Inside Higher Education* http://www.insidehighered.com/news/2007/03/29/accredit.

————. 2008. Margaret Spellings looks back. *Inside Higher Education* http://www.insidehighered.com/news/2008/10/06/spellings.

————. 2009. The senate sheds education aid. *Inside Higher Education.* http://www.insidehighered.com/news/2009/02/09/stimulus.

Lerner, Neal. 2003. Writing center assessment: Searching for the "proof" of our effectiveness. In *The center will hold,* eds. Michael Pemberton and Joyce Kinkead. Logan: Utah State University Press.

Lingenfelter, Paul. 2007. Preface to *More student success: A systemic solution.* Boulder, CO: State Higher Education Executive Officers.

Linn, Robert L. ed. *Educational measurement,* 3rd edition. New York: Macmillian.

Lowe, Teresa J., and Brian Huot. 1997. Using KIRIS writing portfolios to place students in first-year composition at the University of Louisville. *Kentucky English Bulletin* 46 (2): 46–64.

Lynne, Patricia. 2004. *Coming to terms: A theory of writing assessment.* Logan: Utah State University Press.

Mann, Horace. 1891. *Annual reports of the Secretary of the Board of Education of Massachusetts for the years 1837–1838.* Boston: Lee and Shepherd.

Mastrangelo, Lisa. 2010. Lone wolf or leader of the pack?: Rethinking the grand narrative of Fred Newton Scott. *College English* 72: 248–268.

Mayher, John S. 1990. *Uncommon sense: Theoretical practice in language education.* Portsmouth, NH: Boynton/Cook Heinemann.

McPherson, Peter, and David Shulenberger. 2006. Improving student learning in higher education through better accountability and assessment: A discussion paper for the National Association of State Universities and Land-Grant Colleges (NASLGC). http://www.voluntarysystem.org/.

Mehan, Hugh. 1979. *Learning lessons: Social organization in the classroom.* Cambridge: Harvard University Press.

Messick, Samuel. 1989. Meaning and value in test validation: The science and ethics of assessment. *Educational Researcher* 18 (2): 5–11.

————. 1989a. Validity. *Educational Measurement* 3rd Edition, ed. R. L. Linn. Washington DC: Macmillan.

Miller, Charles et al. 2006. *A test of leadership: Charting the future of U.S. Higher Education.* Washington, DC: U.S. Department of Education.

Miller, Susan. 1991. *Textual carnivals: The politics of composition.* Carbondale: Southern Illinois University Press.

Moss, Pamela A. 1992. Shifting conceptions of validity in educational measurement: Implications for performance assessment. *Review of Educational Research* 62 (3).

————. 1994. Can there be validity without reliability?" *Educational Researcher* 23 (4): 5–12.

————. 2007. Joining the dialogue on validity theory in educational research. In O'Neill.

Murphy, Sandra. 2007. Culture and consequences: The canaries in the coal mine. *Research in the Teaching of English* 42: 228–44.

———, and Barbara Grant. 1996. Portfolio approaches to assessment: Breakthrough or more of the same. *Assessment of writing: Politics, policies, practices*, eds. Edward M. White, William D. Lutz, and Sandra Kamusikiri. New York: Modern Language Association.

National Association of State Universities and Land Grant Colleges. 2006. Improving student learning through better accountability and assessment: A discussion paper. Accessed 1/26/2009. http://www.voluntarysystem.org/index.cfm?page=background.

National Center for Educational Achievement. n.d. Overview. http://www.just-4kids.org/en/about_us/partners.cfm .

National Center for Educational Statistics. n.d. *National Assessment of Educational Progress: The nation's report card.* http://nces.ed.gov/nationsreportcard/.

National Commission on Writing. 2003. *The neglected "R": The need for a school revolution.* College Entrance Examination Board.

———.2004. *Writing: A ticket to work . . . or a ticket out.* College Entrance Examination Board.

———.2005. *Writing: A powerful message from state governments.* College Entrance Examination Board.

National Council of Teachers of English. 2004. *NCTE beliefs about the teaching of writing.* http://www.ncte.org/positions/statements/writingbeliefs.

National Council of Teachers of English. 2006. NCTE praises Reading First audit, calls for further investigation. http://www.ncte.org/about/press/key/125668.htm.

National Council of Teachers of English/Council of Writing Program Administrators. 2008. *NCTE-WPA white paper on writing assessment in colleges and universities.* http://wpacouncil.org/white-paper.

Nelson, Alexis. 1999. Views from the underside: Proficiency portfolios in first-year composition. *TETYC* 26: 243–53.

Noble, David W. 1985. *The end of American history.* Minneapolis: University of Minnesota Press.

Noddings, Nell. 2005. *The challenge to care in schools: An alternative approach to education.* New York: Teachers College Press.

Noyes, Ernest C. 1912. Progress in standardizing the measurement of composition. *English Journal* 1: 532–36.

Nunberg, Geoffrey. 2006. *Talking right.* New York: Public Affairs.

Ohanian, Susan. 2007. *NCLB Outrages.* http://www.susanohanian.org/show_nclb_outrages.php?id=2969.

Ohmann, Richard. 2000. Historical reflections on accountability. *Academe Online,* http://aaup.org/AAUP/pubres/academe/2000/JF/Feat/ohmann.

Ondaatje, Michael. 1996. *Billy the kid.* New York: Vintage.

O'Neill, Peggy. 2003. Moving beyond holistic scoring through validity inquiry. *Journal of Writing Assessment* 1 (1): 47–65.

———, ed. 2007. *Blurring boundaries: Developing researchers, writers, and teachers.* Cresskill, NJ: Hampton Press.

———, and Jane Mathison Fife. 1999. Listening to students: Contextualizing response to student writing. *Composition Studies* 27 (2): 39–52.

———, Ellen Schendel, and Brian Huot. 2002. Defining assessment as research: Moving from obligations to opportunities. *WPA: Writing Program Administration* 26 (1/2) :10–26.

———, Sandra Murphy, Brian Huot, and Michael Williamson. 2005. What teachers say about different types of state mandated writing tests. *Journal of writing assessment* 2 (2): 81–108

———, Cindy Moore, and Brian Huot. 2009. *A guide to college writing assessment.* Logan: Utah State University Press.

O'Reilly, Mary Rose. 2005. *The peaceable classroom.* Portsmouth, NH: Boynton/ Cook- Heinemann.

Pagano, Stephen Bernhardt, Dudley Reynolds, Mark Williams, and Matthew Killian McCurrie. 2008. An interinstitutional model for college writing assessment. *College Composition and Communication* 60: 285–320.

Palmer, Orville. 1960. Sixty years of English testing. *College Board* 42 (8): 8–14.

Palmer, Parker. 1998. *The courage to teach: Exploring the inner landscapes of a teacher's life.* San Francisco: Jossey-Bass.

Paris, David. 2006. Higher education at risk? *Inside Higher Education,* http:// www.insidehighered.com/views/2006/10/24/paris.

Parkes, Jay. 2007. Reliability as argument. *Educational Measurement: Issues and Practice* 26 (4):2–10.

Partners in Education Transformation. *Transforming education: Assessing and teaching twenty-first century skills.* Microsoft. http://download.microsoft. com/download/6/E/9/6E9A7CA7-0DC4-4823-993E-A54D18C19F2E/ TransformativeAssessment.pdf.

Perelman, Les. 2009. Information illiteracy and mass market writing assessments. *College Composition and Communication* 60 (1): 128–141.

Perl, Sondra. 1979. The composing processes of unskilled college writers. *Research in the Teaching of English* 13 (4): 317–336.

Perry, Theresa, Claude M Steele, and Asa. G. Hilliard, III. 2003. *Young, gifted and Black: Promoting high achievement among African-American students.* Boston: Beacon Press.

Peters, Brad, and Julie Fisher Robertson. 2007. Portfolio partnerships between faculty and WAC: Lessons from disciplinary practice, reflection, and transformation. *College Composition and Communication* 59: 206–236.

Priddy, Lynn. 2009. Student learning, assessment, and accountability: A complex rubric or uneasy triad. Keynote address for the Council of Writing Program Administrators Annual Meeting, Minneapolis, MN.

Ravitch, Diane. 2010. *The death and life of the great American school system: How testing and choice are undermining education.* New York: Basic Books.

Reese, Stephen D., Oscar H. Gandy, and August E. Grant, eds. 2001. *Framing public life: Perpsectives on media and our understanding of the social world.* LEA Communication Series, edited by Jennings Bryant and Dolf Zillman. Mahwah, NJ: Lawrence Erlbaum.

Rhodes, Terrell. 2009. From the director. *Peer review 11 (1):* 3.

Roemer, Marjorie, Lucille M. Schultz, and Russel K. Durst. 1991. Portfolios and the process of change. *College Composition and Communication* 42: 445–469.

Rose, Mike. 1985. The language of exclusion: Writing instruction in the university. Rep. in *An open language: Selected writing on literacy, learning, and opportunity*. Ed. Mike Rose. Boston: Bedford St. Martins.

———. 1988. Narrowing the mind and page: Remedial writers and cognitive reductionism. *College Composition and Communication* 39 (3): 267-302.

———. 2009. *Why school?: Reclaiming education for all of us*. New York: The New Press.

———. 2010. Writing for the public. *College English* 72 (3): 284–292.

Rose, Shirley, and Irwin Weiser. 2010. *Going public: The WPA as advocate for engagement*. Logan: Utah State University Press.

Ruben, Brent, Laurie Lewis, and Louise Sandmeyer. 2008. *Assessing the impact of the Spellings Commission Report: The message, the messenger, and the dynamics of change in higher education*. Washington, DC: National Association of College and University Business Officers. http://www.nacubo.org:80/documents/business_topics/full%20study.pdf .

Ruth, Leo, and Sandra Murphy. 1984. Designing topics for writing assessment: Problems of meaning. *College Composition and Communication* 35: 410–22.

———. 1988. *Designing writing tasks for the assessment of writing*. Norwood, NJ: Ablex.

Ryan, Charlotte. 1991. *Prime time activism: Media strategies for grassroots organizing*. Boston: South End Press.

Schendel, Ellen. 2000. *Writing assessment as social action*. PhD diss., University of Louisville.

Schubert, William. 1986. *Curriculum: Perspective, paradigm, and possibility*. New York: Macmillan.

Scott, Fred Newton. 1926. *The standard of American speech*. Boston: Allyn and Bacon.

Shepard, Lorrie A. 1993. Evaluating test validity. *Review of Educational Research in Education* 19: 405–50.

———. 2000. The role of assessment in a learning culture. *Educational Researcher* 29 (7): 4–14.

Shupe, David. 2008. Toward a higher standard: The changing organizational context of accountability for educational results. *On the Horizon* 16 (2): 72–96.

Shuy, Roger W. 1981. A holistic view of language. *Research in the Teaching of English* 15: 110–12.

Smith, William L. 1992. The importance of teacher knowledge in college composition placement testing. In *Reading empirical research studies: The rhetoric of research*, ed. John R. Hayes, Norwood, NJ: Ablex.

———. 1993. Assessing the reliability and adequacy of using holistic scoring of essays as a college composition placement technique. In Williamson and Huot.

Soliday, Mary. 2002. *The politics of remediation: Institutional and student needs in higher education*. Pittsburgh: University of Pittsburgh Press.

Sommers, Jeffrey, Laurel Black, Donald Daiker, and Gail Stygall. 1993. The challenges of rating portfolios: What WPAs can expect. *WPA Journal* 17 (1/2): 7–29.

Sommers, Nancy. 1980. Revision strategies of student writers and experienced adult writers. *College Composition and Communication* 31 (4): 378–388.

————. 2009. The call of research: A longitudinal view of writing development. *College Composition and Communication* 60 (1): 152–163.

Sperling, Melanie, and Sarah Freedman. 1987. A good girl writes like a good girl: Written response and clues to the teaching/learning process. *Written Communication* 4: 343–369.

Stanford University Bridge Project. n.d. *Why is P-16 reform necessary?* http://www.stanford.edu/group/bridgeproject/policytoolkit/rationale.html.

Starch, Daniel, and Edward C. Elliott. 1912. Reliability of the grading of high school work in English. *School Review* 20: 442–57.

State Higher Education Executive Officers. 2005. *Accountability for better results: A national imperative for higher education.* Boulder, CO: State Higher Education Executive Officers.

Steele, Claude. M. 1997. A threat in the air: How stereotypes shape the intellectual identities and performance of women and African Americans. *American Psychologist, 52,* 613-629.

Stewart, Donald C., and Patricia L. Stewart. 1997. *The life and legacy of Fred Newton Scott.* Pittsburgh: University of Pittsburgh Press.

Susman, Warren. 1984. *Culture as history.* New York: Pantheon.

Swift, Jonathan. 1789. *A modest proposal.* http://www.gutenberg.org/etext/1080

Szymanski, Daryl. 2009. *Searching for sanctuary in the hazards of high-stakes testing.* Master's project, Eastern Michigan University.

Thaiss, Christopher, and Terry Myers Zawacki. 1997. How portfolios for proficiency help shape a WAC program. In Yancey and Huot.

Thompson, I. 2006. Writing center assessment: Why and a little how. *Writing Center Journal* 26 (1): 33–61.

Thorndike, Edward L. 1931. *Human learning.* New York: The Century Company.

Trachsel, Mary. 1992. *Institutionalizing literacy: The historical role of college entrance exams in English.* Carbondale: Southern Illinois University Press.

Tyack, David. 2003. *Seeking common ground: Public schools in a diverse society.* Cambridge: Harvard University Press.

————, and Larry Cuban. 1995. *Tinkering toward utopia: A century of public school reform.* Cambridge: Harvard University Press.

U.S. Department of Education. 1983. *A Nation at risk: The imperative for education reform.* http://www2.ed.gov/pubs/NatAtRisk/index.html.

Volmer, Jamie. *The blueberry story.* http://www.jamievollmer.com/blue_story.html.

West, Cornel. 1989. *The American evasion of philosophy: A geneology of pragmatism.* Madison: University of Wisconsin Press.

White, Edward M. 1993. Holistic scoring: Past triumphs and future challenges. In Williamson and Huot.

————. 2005. The scoring of portfolios: Phase 2. *College Composition and Communication* 56: 581–600.

Willard-Traub, Margaret, Emily Decker, Rebecca Reed, and Jerome Johnston. 1999. The development of large-scale portfolio placement at the University of Michigan 1992–1998. *Assessing Writing* 6: 41–84.

Williams, Raymond. 1973. Base and superstructure in Marxist cultural theory. *New Left Review* 1 (82): 1–10.

Williamson, Michael M. 1993. An introduction to holistic scoring: The social, historical and context for writing assessment. In Williamson and Huot.

——. 1994. The worship of efficiency: Untangling theoretical and practical considerations in writing assessment. *Assessing Writing* 1:147–74.

Williamson, Michael M., and Brian A. Huot, eds. 1993. *Validating holistic scoring: Theoretical and empirical foundations.* Cresskill, NJ: Hampton Press.

Wise, Gene. 1980. *American historical explanations: A strategy for grounded inquiry.* Minneapolis: University of Minnesota Press.

Witte, Stephen P., Mary Traschel, and Keith Walters. 1987. Literacy and direct assessment of writing: A diachronic perspective. In *Writing assessment: Issues and strategies,* eds. Karen L. Greenberg, Harvey S. Weiner, and Richard A. Donovan. New York: Longman.

Yancey, Kathleen Blake. 1999. Looking back as we look forward: Historicizing writing assessment." *College Composition and Communication* 50: 483-503.

——, and Brian Huot, eds. 1997. *Assessing writing across the curriculum: diverse approaches and practices. Perspectives on writing: theory, research, practice.* Greenwich, CT: Ablex.

INDEX

ABOUT THE AUTHORS

Since getting to know each other through work with the WPA Network for Media Action, Linda Adler-Kassner and Peggy O'Neill have collaborated on issues related to writing assessment, public policy, and writing instruction.

LINDA ADLER-KASSNER is professor of writing and director of the writing program at University of California, Santa Barbara, where she teaches undergraduate and graduate writing courses. Through 2011, she is also the President of the Council of Writing Program Administrators and served an additional five years on the Executive Board of that organization, including working as founding coordinator of the WPA Network for Media Action. Most recently, her research has focused both on analyzing the implications of public policy for writing instruction, and on developing strategies for writing instructors and program directors to affect policy. She is also author of *The Activist WPA: Changing Stories about Writers and Writing* (Utah State University Press 2008), and co-author or co-editor of six additional books. She also has published many articles and book chapters in journals such as *College Composition and Communication, WPA Journal,* and *Journal of Basic Writing.*

PEGGY O'NEILL, associate professor, directs the composition program and teaches writing and rhetoric courses in the department of writing at Loyola University, Maryland. Her scholarship focuses primarily on writing assessment and pedagogy. Her work appears in academic journals, such as the *Journal of Writing Assessment* and *College Composition and Communication,* as well as in several edited scholarly collections. Her most recent book is *A Guide to College Writing Assessment* (Utah State University Press 2009), which she co-authored with Cindy Moore and Brian Huot. O'Neill has also edited or co-edited four books: *Assessing Writing: A Critical Sourcebook* (Bedford St. Martin's / NCTE 2009); *Blurring Boundaries: Developing Writers, Researchers and Teachers* (Hampton Press 2007); *A Field of Dreams: Independent Writing Programs and the Future of Composition Studies* (Utah State University Press 2002); and *Practice in Context: Situating the Work of Writing Teachers* (NCTE 2002).